Book of the New American Nation

BROWN PAPER SCHOOL
USKids History: Book of the New American Nation

Written by Marlene Smith-Baranzini *and* Howard Egger-Bovet

James J. Rawls, *Consulting Editor*

Illustrated by T. Taylor Bruce

Little, Brown and Company

Boston   New York   Toronto   London

A Yolla Bolly Press Book **RAP** 3474733√

Brown Paper School USKids History: Book of the New American Nation was edited and prepared for publication at The Yolla Bolly Press, Covelo, California. This series is under the supervision of James Robertson and Carolyn Robertson. Production staff: Diana Fairbanks, Renée Menge, and Alexandra Chappell. Composition by Wilsted & Taylor, Oakland, California.

FIRST EDITION

MV-NY

Published simultaneously in Canada by Little, Brown & Company (Canada) Limited

Printed in the United States of America

Library of Congress Cataloging-in-Publication Data

Smith-Baranzini, Marlene.
    USKids history. Book of the new American nation / written by Marlene Smith-Baranzini and Howard Egger-Bovet ; illustrated by T. Taylor Bruce. — 1st ed.
        p.   cm. — (Brown paper school)
    "A Yolla Bolly Press book"
    Includes bibliographical references and index.
    ISBN 0-316-96923-0 (hc)
    ISBN 0-316-22206-2 (pbk)
    1. United States—History—1783–1865—Juvenile literature.
[1. United States—History—1783–1865.] I. Egger-Bovet, Howard.   II. Bruce, T. Taylor, ill.   III. Title.   IV. Title: USKids history. Book of the new American nation.   V. Title: Book of the new American nation.   VI. Series.
E301.S58   1995
973.5—dc20   94-13075

Contents

Note: Activities and games are italicized.

The Plowboy and His Book

On the cover of this book is a picture of a boy who is guiding a plow through a field. We don't know his real name, but we will call him Samuel. The field that Samuel is plowing is in the Ohio Territory, miles from the nearest neighbor. It is early on a morning in May, 1787, late in the year to be plowing. The wildflowers are already up. But before Samuel could plow his field, the trees that covered it had to be cut down. Samuel's father and his brothers used them to build their log house. Now the field must be plowed and planted so that Samuel, his family, and their animals will have food for the duration of the long Ohio winter.

Samuel and his family are settlers. They and many families just like them loaded their belongings into carts and wagons and left the cities and villages of the new nation in search of good farmland. Americans had won their war for independence. Soon after, many thousands of people began to move west into the territories of Ohio, Indiana, and Kentucky. They were eager to claim the land they had fought for and won.

But whose land was it really? For many centuries, American Indians had lived in the western territories and thought that the land was in their care. They asked, How can a person own the soil, the wild animals, the trees, and the water and the sun that give life? These are things that belong to all people. No single person can own them. As white settlers moved west in larger and larger numbers, Indians were forced to make many changes in their lives. Though some Indians welcomed their new neighbors, others fought the whites. For every friendship, there were many battles. It was the beginning of a long period of much trouble and sadness.

It was also a time of great excitement and accomplishments for the new American nation. On the very day that Samuel was plowing his field in the Ohio Territory, men were gathering in Philadelphia. They were there to form a new government. They would write our Constitution. Later, they would elect our first president. Later still, a black man would survey 300 acres along the Potomac River for the nation's new capital.

By the time Samuel was a young man with a family of his own, the new American nation was growing. Our third president had purchased the Louisiana Territory, a huge tract of land, from France. Soon after that, two brave explorers and their men would travel thousands of miles by boat and on foot and would see

things no other white men had seen as they made their way to the Pacific Ocean.

You will read about all these events and many others in this book. Now look once again at the picture on the cover. If you look carefully, you will see that Samuel has a book tied to his plow. There were no schools for Samuel to attend in May of 1787. Samuel knew that his future depended upon how much he could learn. And since he was needed on his family's new farm, he would learn as much and whenever he could.

We don't know what became of Samuel. But if you look back far enough at your own family, you are apt to find a Samuel, or a Samantha, or a Patrick, very likely from some other land, or perhaps from an Indian nation, who taught himself or herself to read, and became a citizen of the new American nation. The history of our country is also the history of you.

A Wild Mississippi Scheme

Patsy looked at her father in amazement.

Patsy Jefferson sat at the mahogany table in the boardinghouse on Second Street. She pretended to concentrate on her supper. With her pewter fork, she poked at the chunks of boiled mutton and sausage that were left on her plate. She hoped her father—if he noticed at all—would think she was still eating. Mrs. House, the elderly woman with whom the Jeffersons were staying, began clearing the serving platters.

In its birdcage near the dining room window, Patsy's parrot, Thadwell, squawked. The bird had belonged to her mother, who had died in 1782 after a long illness. Since then, whenever Thomas Jefferson brought his eleven-year-old daughter with him to Philadelphia from their home in Virginia, he always brought Thadwell, too.

Thomas Jefferson glanced at Patsy and smiled. He filled Mrs. Trist's wineglass and then his own. He was about to speak when Mrs. Trist made her surprising announcement.

"Now that the peace agreement has been signed," she said, "I can finally leave Philadelphia. I have waited *months* for this event."

Patsy looked at her father in amazement. She could not leave the table *now*.

Jefferson leaned forward, resting an elbow on the arm of his chair, with an expression of concern on his face. As always when he discussed serious matters, he seemed to forget his eldest daughter was present. Patsy loved listening to him.

"Indeed, Eliza, the fighting in America is over. Our peace treaty with Britain, France, and Spain has been signed. In the agreement, the land along the lower Mississippi has been divided between America and Spain. I know you long to see Nicholas, so far away in Louisiana. But let him come to you. The Mississippi River"—Jefferson's voice rose, paused, and continued—"cuts through unsettled, dangerous land. The journey would be perilous beyond imagination."

Mrs. Trist reached over and took Jefferson's hand.

"My dear friend," she said, smiling, "I have waited for your visit to tell you this. You know my husband has acquired plantation land in the South. I *must* go. But I assure you, I am doing nothing risky. Alexander Fowler, his close friend, has already agreed to travel with me to Fort Pitt. He knows of a company in Pittsburgh that will have a strong flatboat built for us by early spring. And you remember my cousin Polly? She will accompany me the entire distance. With such companions, I will manage nicely."

Then Elizabeth looked at Patsy, who seemed like a daughter to her. "And I have a woman friend who would be delighted to care for Patsy while you are here in the city."

"So you have been at this wild Mississippi scheme for some time, I see," Jefferson replied at last. "I wish I could persuade you to reconsider. If I cannot, I will offer any assistance you might need."

Patsy shook her chestnut-brown hair from her shoulders and sat taller. Seven years of war were over. She was glad that the colonies—now called states—had won the battle for independence. When the fighting ended last winter, her father had allowed her to come to Philadelphia while he attended Congress. This was her second trip to the city. Now, she realized, peace meant that Mrs. Trist, too, could travel wherever she wanted to go.

Patsy had expected Mr. Trist to return to his family after the war, never thinking that his wife might leave instead. Since her mother's death, Patsy liked living in the big red brick house while her father attended Congress. Mrs. Trist ordered new dresses for her, she liked her French tutor, there were always guests to meet, and she loved her little bedroom on the third floor.

Patsy wanted Mrs. Trist to be with her husband again, too. But couldn't she go some other time?

Elizabeth Trist's first day on the Ohio was easy.

A JOURNEY DOWN THE OHIO AND MISSISSIPPI RIVERS

Elizabeth Trist knew that Thomas Jefferson was curious about the little-known lands to the west. She kept a travel diary of her voyage, writing to him about the unusual things she saw. Her diary was found in 1987. It tells us that in January 1784, she and a woman named Polly left Philadelphia on horseback. Traveling with a small group, they rode through deep winter snows. They crossed the Allegheny Mountains and several icy rivers. When they reached Pittsburgh, she and Polly waited while the weather improved and their flatboat was finished. When the boat was finally ready, they began the journey down two of the biggest rivers known in America at that time, the Ohio and the Mississippi. This is an account of her river trip. In the quotations from her diary, her spelling has not been changed.

Elizabeth Trist's first day on the Ohio River was easy. She enjoyed the scenery as the flatboat drifted along on the current. It was May 20, 1784. Someone said they had gone thirty miles since leaving Pittsburgh at noon. As sunset faded on the horizon, she finished her tea and prepared for bed. She wondered how many weeks until she would arrive in Natchez, Mississippi.

Elizabeth climbed up onto her sleeping berth to dress for bed. The ceiling was low. As she leaned back to fold up her skirt, the boat swayed. She toppled backward and tumbled to the deck with a thud.

Polly's eyes flew open as she slid out of bed to help her fallen companion. Elizabeth had bumped her head and hit her shoulder. She was all right, but she had hurt herself "sufficient to make me a little more carefull in future." She fell asleep realizing that riverboating might take some getting used to.

Three days later Elizabeth discovered that when it rained she must expect to be drenched. "A very severe shower . . . has wet our beding," she wrote. Thunder, lightning, and heavy rain made the night "dreadfull." The roof leaked in several places.

As they traveled, the boat stopped often so the men could hunt deer, pheasant, or anything they could shoot for food. They were not always lucky. On May 23, 1784, Elizabeth wrote, "We have not seen any wild beasts till today a bear presented himself to our view; but he made off before our people cou'd get a fire at him. . . .

The boat stopped often so the men could hunt.

There are such numbers of boats continually going down the river," she added, "that all the game have left the shore."

Later she wrote, "Our people kill'd a tame cow which they mistook for a Buffaloe." Another afternoon, the men hunted for turtle eggs. The search failed, but they came back with a "fine Gosling." Somewhere along the route, Elizabeth was given a little dog. She named her new pet Fawnis.

The voyage became difficult near Louisville, where the Ohio River entered a narrow channel of waterfalls and swift rapids. The men who owned the flatboat were not skilled enough to navigate the unpredictable river. The current gave the boat a strong jolt and suddenly it was wedged among the rocks. According to Elizabeth's diary, no one was happy with the pilot's steering ability. "Either his villany or carelessness run her [the boat] onto the Rocks," she said. The owners were forced to hire an experienced river pilot who could free the boat and guide it safely through the dangerous water.

But the boat had to be unloaded before the new pilot could move it off the rocks. While the

Flatboats on the River

In the late 1700s, traveling by river was the easiest and cheapest way to cover a long distance. Flatboats were flat-bottomed barges that drifted with the current, carrying people and cargo. Since they couldn't drift *against* the current, they were good for only one-way travel. They were steered by long poles, called "sweeps," attached at the top of the boat.

Most flatboats were built in Pittsburgh, to travel on the Ohio and Mississippi Rivers. A typical flatboat was fifty feet long, but only fifteen feet wide, so it could pass through narrow channels in the Ohio River.

Flatboats were made of long planks, often including a six-foot-high "fence" with portholes around the outer deck as protection against an attack from shore. One end was covered with a roof, which provided a sheltered area for sleeping and eating.

When flatboats reached their destination, they were taken apart. The lumber was used again, often to build new homes for some of the passengers.

river men worked, the passengers found shelter at an abandoned fort. The rapids delayed their journey by eight days.

On an average day, the current could carry the flatboat thirty miles. When the wind blew from behind, the boat drifted faster, sometimes making fifty miles a day.

Once the boat entered a channel where the waters formed a strong whirlpool. "Our boat went round like a top," Elizabeth wrote. Other boats were not so lucky at this spot. Someone told her that just a year ago, a boat carrying 600 barrels of flour had sunk after it collided with a pile of abandoned lumber in the water.

On June 13, 1784, the flatboat left the Ohio River and entered the Mississippi, the "Grand Riviere," Elizabeth called it, using her French. Near the rivers' junction, she was delighted to discover Fort Jefferson, built during the Revolutionary War and named in honor of her friend Thomas. It had been taken over by Indians—she called them Taumas—from farther north in Ohio. She wanted to see the fort, but no one on the flatboat knew how the Indians might treat them.

In some places along the Mississippi, the riverbank stood fifty feet above the water. Its steep walls were colored deep red with iron ore and were very ragged. The signs of erosion caused Elizabeth to write that "great pieces of earth [tumble] into the water." Trees from the banks were often uprooted, filling the river with logs.

Elizabeth and Polly were deep into territory where the landforms, trees, and even animals were strange and new. One of the men killed a large white bird with black-tipped wings. It was

brought onto the boat. Elizabeth studied it so she could describe it for Jefferson. "They are a fine Majestick looking bird and at a distance resemble a swan. The Bill is about an inch wide and a foot in length. The underjaw . . . resembles leather and expands in an extraordanary manner." The passengers gathered around to watch as the men poured fourteen quarts of water into its mouth. "I cannot comprehend what use they make of this amaizing pouch," she wrote, "unless to scoop up the little fish." The pelican was "the most curious bird I ever saw," Elizabeth declared.

She soon discovered a more dangerous creature. On June 29, the flatboat stopped at an island for the night. The dog Fawnis was missing. Elizabeth searched everywhere, without success. "Tis supposed the Allegator got him," she wrote sadly, "as one was seen swimming about the boat in the evening—poor little fellow."

Finally, on July 1, Elizabeth Trist could write, "My journey is almost compleated. Three days more and I shall be happy in sight of Natchez." Natchez, Mississippi, was a small community of about 500 people. There the flatboat would dock and, for several days, would unload its cargo of flour. Now Elizabeth would send a letter to her husband in Louisiana and tell him she had arrived.

It would be a long time before Elizabeth Trist returned to Philadelphia. As soon as she could, she would send her little diary to Thomas Jefferson. But for now, she closed it and packed it away.

The current could carry the flatboat thirty miles in a day.

Build a Model Flatboat

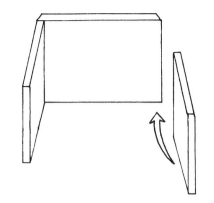

Nail the three 5-by-3-inch pieces together to make a "U" shape. These are the walls.

Nail the roof to the walls.

Nail the shelter to the base from the bottom.

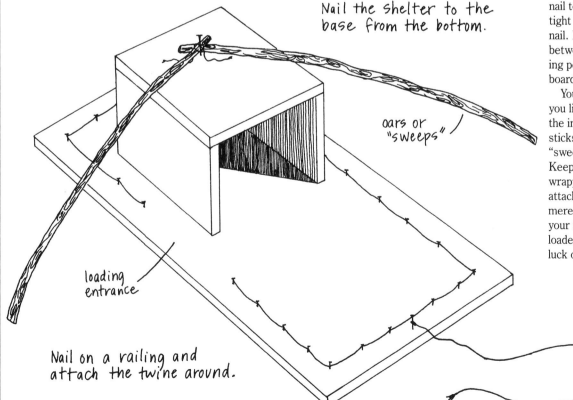

oars or "sweeps"

loading entrance

Nail on a railing and attach the twine around.

Look at the flatboat picture that accompanies Mrs. Trist's diary. Can you guess why flatboats were easier to build than other kinds of watercraft? You can make one to carry action figures or a small doll family and some farm animals. Let it drift on a creek, a lake, or even the ocean.

You Will Need:

A hammer; nails; twine; and five scraps of wood, 7 by 12 inches, 5 by 5 inches, and three pieces that are 5 by 3 inches. The largest wood piece will be the base. Three should be the same size, for the sides of the shelter. The fifth piece will be the roof of the shelter.

1. To make the covered area, arrange the same-size pieces of wood in a "U" shape and nail them together at the corners.

2. Cover this shelter with a piece of wood and nail it down, hammering through the roof and into the shelter.

3. To make the base, turn the shelter upside down and place the largest piece of wood over it. Nail the base to the shelter. Turn it upright and check to see that it's nailed down firmly.

4. Attach a long piece of twine to the front of the flatboat so you can pull it through the water. To do this, hammer a long nail into the front center of the base. Tie one end of the twine tightly around the nail. If you want a railing around the boat, hammer a row of nails around the base, keeping the nails about an inch apart and ½ inch inside the edge of the base. Wrap twine from one nail to the next, making a tight loop around each nail. Leave an entrance between two nails for loading people and animals on board.

Your flatboat is done. If you like, make furniture for the inside and add two sticks (for oars, called "sweeps") to the roof. Keep them in place by wrapping them with twine attached to a nail hammered into the roof. Now your flatboat is ready to be loaded and launched. Good luck on your journey!

Mississippi Trist

Discover the adventures that awaited flatboat travelers like Elizabeth Trist. Follow these instructions to make a game board of the Ohio and Mississippi Rivers and a set of river cards to guide players. Round up any number of friends, roll the dice, and drift away! The first player to land at Natchez, Mississippi, wins the game.

You Will Need:

A sheet of white poster board, 11 by 17 inches; a pencil; a yardstick; a black marker; crayons or colored markers; ten 3 by 5–inch index cards; a ruler; a die; and six rectangles of wood or clay, 1 by ½ by ¾ inches, each colored or marked differently, to serve as flatboats.

1. With the yardstick and pencil, draw a grid dividing the poster board into 1-inch squares. Number twenty-three squares as they are numbered in the illustration here. Using the map in this book as a guide, draw the Ohio and Mississippi Rivers on the poster board. Begin the Ohio River in square 1 and end the Mississippi River in square 23. Make sure you copy the river route so it crosses through each numbered square.

2. Outline the rivers, the twenty-three game squares, and the game square numbers in black marker.

3. Finish the board by drawing and coloring trees, hills, forts, rapids, and sandbars on or beside the rivers.

4. Cut the index cards in half (3 by 2½ inches) to make river cards. Print the word *Progress* on ten cards and *Pitfall* on the other ten. Turn the Progress cards over and print one set of the following instructions on each card:

Strong tailwinds. Move ahead four spaces.

Hunting along shore is plentiful. Roll die and take an extra turn.

Flatboat captain is very careful. Move ahead two spaces.

Friendly passenger helps navigate. Move ahead one space.

Flatboat is carried on swift current. Move ahead two spaces.

Captain sells off extra cargo. Flatboat is lighter. Roll die and take an extra turn.

Settlers living along shore tell captain of shortcut fork in river. Take an extra turn.

Expert river pilot guides flatboat safely through rapids. Skip ahead three spaces.

Flatboats ahead clear fallen trees from river. Advance one space.

Doctor on board treats injured passengers without needing to stop. Skip ahead one space.

5. Write one set of these instructions on the back of each Pitfall card:

Severe thunderstorm forces captain to tie up at shore. Skip next turn.

Captain accidentally steers boat to west side of Mississippi River, which is Spanish Territory. Lose one turn.

Hunters find no sign of game along river. Skip next turn.

While flatboat is tied at fort, rope frays and boat drifts downriver. Lose a turn.

No wind for three days. Go back two spaces.

Narrow channel in river. Six flatboats ahead, waiting to pass. Lose next turn.

Flatboat stops for supplies at Louisville. Two passengers return late, delaying departure. Lose one turn.

Flatboat hits hidden rocks. Repairs take one week. Lose next two turns.

Captain stops to sketch pelicans beside river. Go back one space.

Swarm of alligators blocks river ahead. Lose next turn.

How You Play:

Place flatboats at top of game board near Pittsburgh and river cards in separate stacks where all players can reach them. To begin, each player rolls the die. The player with the highest number places a flatboat on square 1, rolls the die, and moves the number of spaces indicated on the die. Players take turns rolling the die and advancing toward Natchez.

The following special conditions apply to certain numbers and situations: Whenever a 2 is rolled, the player who rolled it picks a Progress card from the top of the deck and follows its instructions. (The card is then returned to the bottom of the deck.) Whenever a 4 is rolled, the player who rolled it takes a Pitfall card from the top of the deck and follows its instructions. (The card is

The Board Game

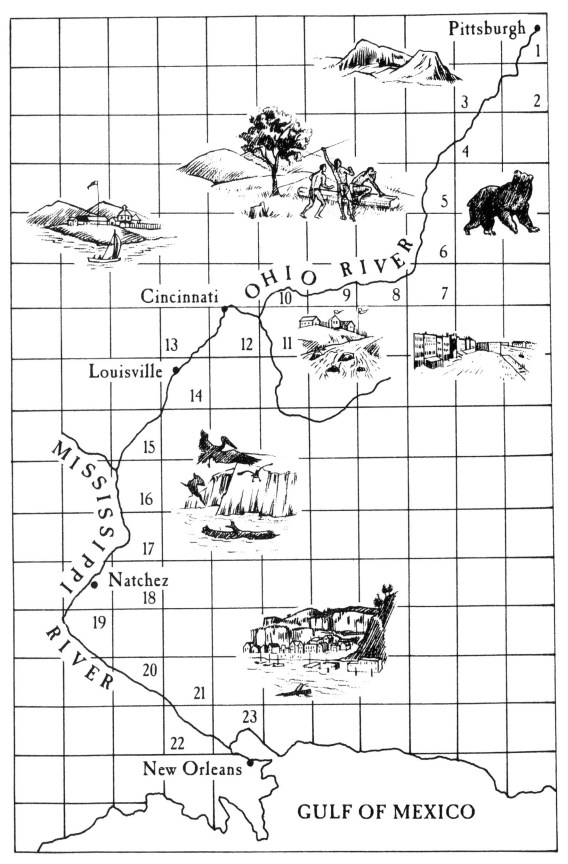

then returned to the bottom of the deck.) When any player rolls a 5 in two successive turns, he or she may, *if desired*, automatically advance two extra spaces. When any player chooses a Progress card that instructs him or her to roll again, and on the next roll the player rolls a 2 or a 4, the player moves ahead two or four spaces but does not take another river card.

The first player to land at Natchez by rolling the exact number of squares wins the game. When any player rolls a high number and passes Natchez, that player automatically returns to square 15. On the player's next turn, he or she rolls again and tries to land on Natchez. If that player rolls any number other than a 3, he or she may skip that turn and stay on square 15 until the next turn, hoping to roll a 1, 2, or 3 to try and win. Also, if a player near Natchez rolls a 2 and the Progress card instructs the player to move beyond Natchez, that player may follow instructions and advance, and on the next turns choose Pitfall cards instead of rolling the die (hoping the Pitfall cards will instruct the player to move back to Natchez and win the game). Or the player may choose to go directly to square 15 and wait for his or her next turn.

What Did You Learn in School Today?

Have you ever wondered why you go to school every day, or why you learn certain things and not others? Do you know who decides what your school will teach? These are questions that don't have easy answers. But asking them is a smart thing to do.

Two hundred years ago, children didn't have to go to school. Parents decided if their children would go to school and where, because they had to pay for their children's education. Many parents wanted their children to learn to read for only one reason: so they could study the Bible. Sometimes it was the only book a family owned.

Very wealthy families could send their children to school in England or France, to study for months or years at a time. Or a group of families who lived in the country might hire one tutor to teach all the children in the neighborhood. As the sons of the rich became teenagers, they went on to college. Girls learned the skills and arts they would need to be wives and mothers, manage a house, and entertain guests.

City children usually started at a "dame school," called that because it was taught by a woman. After they knew the alphabet and how to read, they could go on to grammar school. Boys would often take up their father's line of work or learn a trade by watching and helping an uncle.

Many ordinary people and poor families did not have money to pay a teacher. More important than that, they needed every child at home to help with the work.

SPELLE IT RYGHTE

Noah Webster

Did you notice how Elizabeth Trist spelled *carefull* and *dreadfull* in her travel diary? If she had been a student in Noah Webster's classroom, she would have erased the final *l* in both words. Why? Too British, cried Webster. He insisted—and most people agreed—that it was time Americans had new rules for using their language in a country that wasn't British anymore.

In 1782 Noah Webster was a patriotic young teacher with his first classroom. The one thing he disliked about school was the books. They all came from England. Webster wanted American children to learn about American life from schoolbooks written by Americans. The "Empire of America," as he called it, should not get its books from a "foreign Kingdom." Webster especially wanted all Americans to spell words the "American" way.

To make this possible, in 1783 Webster wrote and published an American speller. The *Blue-Backed Speller* was an instant hit and made him famous. It cost 14¢, and children everywhere had copies. When families moved north, south, east, or west, the little book went with them. It was popular for more than a hundred years and sold more than 100 million copies.

Webster did more than any other person to create a single standard for writing American English. To go with his new spelling book—or was it because he soon had six children running around at home?—he added a grammar and a reader. Then, with so many new words created by life in America, Webster tackled a huge project: he wrote the first American dictionary. You may even have a modern version of Webster's dictionary at home or in school.

These are some of the ABC lessons in Webster's spelling book.

Short a: The first m*a*n was *A*dam, *a*nd the first woman was Eve. The m*a*n cuts down trees with his *a*x.

Long a: Oak trees produce *a*corns, and little animals eat them. Girls wear *a*prons to keep their frocks clean.

B: Girls are fond of fine *b*eads to wear round their necks. *B*ears live in the woods. Some fish are very *b*ony. *B*ad *b*oys love to rob the nests of *b*irds.

Hard c: A *c*utlass is a broad *c*urving sword. He had a new red *c*ap.

Soft c: A *c*itadel is a fortress to defend a *c*ity or town. One dollar is one hundred *c*ents. Never go into a barn or stable with a lighted *c*igar in your mouth; and it will be better still if you never have a *c*igar in your mouth at all.

If you want to see the rest of the alphabet, ask if your library has a revised version of *The Blue-Backed Speller*, which is now called *The American Speller*.

Living on Someone Else's Land

Darting Eyes proudly stared at her father.

It was a spring night; the moon was just a sliver in the sky. Into this night traveled a raiding party from a Cherokee village.

It was not a long journey. The men moved through wildflowers and into the woods given to them by the Great Spirit. They passed trees that had been marked by white settlers. The marks meant this land was now claimed by the settlers. The Indians did not understand the meaning of these marks. Nor did the settlers understand the meaning of the Great Spirit.

The raiding party could see the settlement. They saw ten new cabins under construction. That brought the total to thirty cabins in all. There seemed to be no end to the growth of this white settlement.

The Cherokee men knew what they had to do. They left the protection of the forest's shadow and attacked the settlement. Women and children ran from their houses toward the safety of the nearby fort. Men grabbed their muskets to defend their homes.

The Cherokee raiding party destroyed cabins, turned over wagons, and attacked settlers. The white men fired their muskets and reloaded as quickly as they could. The Cherokee men, some badly wounded, jumped onto the settlers' horses and raced to their village.

The Cherokee men were welcomed back. Later, as they sat around the fire, a girl, nicknamed Darting Eyes, proudly stared at her father. His forehead and left arm were covered in blood. It was not the first time she had seen her father wounded. Many of the men in the village were covered in a tapestry of scars from previous battles with white settlers.

Darting Eyes stared out toward the woods. A cold chill ran through her body. Soon, perhaps tomorrow, the white men would attack her village for what the raiding party had done tonight. This meant her father and the other men would attack the white settlers again. It was a war. Darting Eyes wondered if it would ever end.

Americans Couldn't Wait

The Revolutionary War was over. The Americans had defeated the British forces. After losing the war, the British king no longer had the right to rule Americans. The British also gave up the rights to a huge region known as the Northwest Territory. This land was situated west of Pennsylvania, east of the Mississippi River, and north of the Ohio River.

The American Congress assumed the right to approve citizens settling on this land. But many citizens had no patience to wait for Congress's approval. They lived illegally on land inhabited by Indian people. Their presence on Indian land soon led to many bloody conflicts.

Tecumseh rode west, urging the people to unite.

Good Intentions

The United States Congress stated, "The utmost good faith shall always be observed towards the Indian, their land and property shall never be taken from them without their consent. . . ."

A Dollar an Acre

In 1785 Congress established rules for how the Northwest Territory would be settled. The land would be divided into sections. Each section would be one-square mile, or 640 acres. Six sections would make up a town.

There was a problem. The minimum purchase was 640 acres, which cost $640! Farmers couldn't afford to buy that much land. Men with money, called land speculators, quickly bought up huge tracts of land. They sold smaller sections of land to farmers for a profit.

People on the Move

Major John Doughty was stationed at Fort Harmar, which was located on the Muskingum River in what is now Ohio. It was common for him to see people traveling down the river by flatboat or barge to make a home in the Northwest Territory. Between April 6 and May 16, 1788, Major John Doughty was so amazed by the volume of this migration that he wrote it down: "181 boats, 406 souls [people], 1,588 horses, 314 horned cattle, 223 sheep, and 92 wagons."

THE PEACEMAKER AND THE PROPHET

The great Shawnee war chief Tecumseh watched his people lose their land. He had been born in 1768, on the Mad River in western Ohio. He saw many treaties made and broken. The land, he said, was like the sea and the air. It cannot be sold.

Tecumseh thought about what would help the Indians. In 1806 he and his younger brother Tenskwatawa, who was called "the Prophet," began to see that if all Indian tribes joined together, they could keep the land they still had.

For two years, Tecumseh rode through the west on horseback, from the Great Lakes to the Gulf of Mexico, urging the Indian people to unite into a larger nation. He held a vision of a separate Indian nation where the people lived in peace and their lifeways were respected. Tenskwatawa inspired them to live wisely and honor the Great Spirit.

Some tribes recognized the brothers' wisdom and joined with them. But too many others wondered why they should.

Tecumseh asked the Indians to be humane to their enemies in battle. White leaders called him "the Peacemaker" and praised him for following his own advice. Some men said he was the greatest Indian who ever lived.

The governor of the Indiana Territory called Chief Tecumseh an "uncommon genius." Yet the governor wanted the Indians to leave the lands north of the Ohio River and east of the Mississippi River, called the Northwest Territory. The Shawnee chief refused to be driven away.

The Indians turned to the British for help. After the Revolutionary War, many British had left the new United States and settled in Canada. Now they were fighting with the Americans over which nation would control the Ohio country and the Mississippi River valley. Tecumseh and his followers joined with the British against the Americans.

Although the War of 1812 was not a true victory for either nation, the Americans forced the British and Indians to retreat into Canada. Among them was Tecumseh. In October 1813 he was killed by American soldiers at the Battle of the Thames. Without their great chief, his followers lost heart and gave up hope. Tecumseh's dream of Indian unity was dead.

THE UNITED STATES, 1787

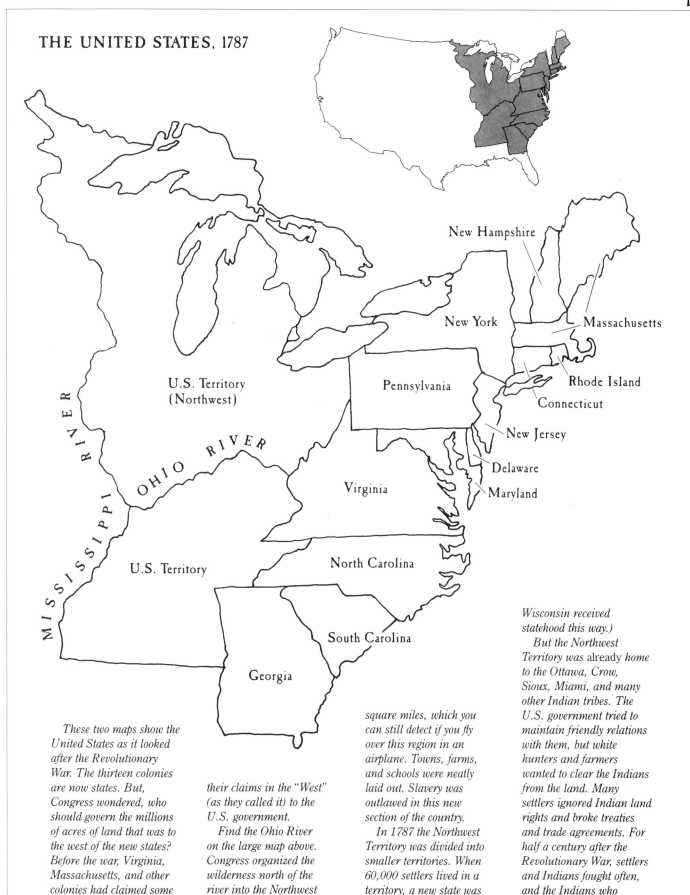

New Hampshire

New York

Massachusetts

Rhode Island

Connecticut

Pennsylvania

New Jersey

Delaware

Maryland

U.S. Territory
(Northwest)

Virginia

North Carolina

U.S. Territory

South Carolina

Georgia

MISSISSIPPI RIVER

OHIO RIVER

These two maps show the United States as it looked after the Revolutionary War. The thirteen colonies are now states. But, Congress wondered, who should govern the millions of acres of land that was to the west of the new states? Before the war, Virginia, Massachusetts, and other colonies had claimed some of the land. By 1786, the colonies decided to give their claims in the "West" (as they called it) to the U.S. government.

Find the Ohio River on the large map above. Congress organized the wilderness north of the river into the Northwest Territory. The land was surveyed into a grid of square miles, which you can still detect if you fly over this region in an airplane. Towns, farms, and schools were neatly laid out. Slavery was outlawed in this new section of the country.

In 1787 the Northwest Territory was divided into smaller territories. When 60,000 settlers lived in a territory, a new state was created. (Michigan, Ohio, Indiana, Illinois, and Wisconsin received statehood this way.)

But the Northwest Territory was already home to the Ottawa, Crow, Sioux, Miami, and many other Indian tribes. The U.S. government tried to maintain friendly relations with them, but white hunters and farmers wanted to clear the Indians from the land. Many settlers ignored Indian land rights and broke treaties and trade agreements. For half a century after the Revolutionary War, settlers and Indians fought often, and the Indians who survived were pushed farther and farther west.

Jason's Secret

Jason moved from table to table, pouring the water.

In 1776 the members of Congress wrote the Articles of Confederation. This plan created a confederation, or a loose union of independent colonies. The confederation worked well enough during the Revolutionary War. Everyone was united to rid the colonies of British rule.

But after the war was over, this loose form of government led to many problems. Some states refused to accept money printed in other states. States disagreed over where their borders were. There were conflicts over trade. Congress was helpless to settle these conflicts, because it had no real power over the states.

On May 25, 1787, delegates from the thirteen states gathered in Philadelphia to try to solve these and other problems.

It was hot in Philadelphia. Jason hurried down Market Street. It was crowded with shoppers buying everything from tea to cloth to snapping turtles.

"Did you know James Madison of Virginia is here for the convention?" asked one man.

"He's been here for almost two weeks, and he hasn't said a word to anyone," replied another shopper. "He just studies and writes. The other delegates have been just as silent."

"Jason!" called his friend Patrick. "Come and look at this turtle. It almost bit my finger off!"

"I can't," said Jason, not bothering to stop.

"You're going to the State House, aren't you?" asked his friend, chasing after him. "What are the delegates doing over there?"

"I don't know."

"Your father is guarding the convention room, and he hasn't told you anything?"

"No! Now go back to your turtles."

Jason's father hadn't said a word to his son. All his son knew was that his father was guarding some of America's most important men. Benjamin Franklin was at the convention, and so was George Washington.

Jason turned right up Chestnut Street. He walked into the State House and stood in the great hallway. At the back, his father signaled him to come quickly. He ran to him.

"Now, listen to me," said his father. "The delegates are thirsty. I told them you could be trusted to bring them water. Can you keep a secret, even from me?"

"From you!"

"Yes. Whatever you hear in there cannot be repeated to anyone, not even to me."

Jason agreed. He walked to the well at the corner of Chestnut Street. He drew water into a bucket. He returned to the State House.

His father opened the door and said, "Lock the door behind you and don't say a word."

Jason stepped inside and locked the door. The air in the large room was hot and stale. The windows were shut and the blinds were drawn.

Jason paid no attention to the delegates sitting at thirteen library tables. He looked up at the speakers' platform. Behind a desk, sitting in an armchair, was the president of the convention, George Washington. Jason stared at his hero.

"My goodness, he's tall," thought Jason.

Jason moved from table to table, pouring the water. He tried not to listen, but it was impossible. He heard the words "Virginia Plan," and "There must be one supreme power. . . ." He heard talk of overthrowing the government!

Shocked by what he heard, Jason poured the last of the water. Did the delegates really mean

to overthrow the government? Was this supreme power a king? Had the delegates gathered to choose an American king?

Jason left the room bursting to tell his father what he had heard. There was evil work going on in there. His father glared at him. Jason said nothing and walked back to the well. Patrick was waiting for him there.

"Jason," said Patrick, "what are you doing? Have you been inside? What are they saying in there?"

"I can't tell you," he said.

Jason desperately wanted to speak to his friend. He bit his lip, filled the bucket, and walked away.

He continued to serve water almost every day for the next four months. He no longer believed what the delegates were doing was evil, but he still didn't understand all he had heard.

The delegates argued and argued. Two delegates had enough and left. There was talk about a head of government, how long he should serve, and a legislature with two houses.

Jason was confused. Each state already had a head of government and a legislature. What was all the fuss about? Why couldn't he tell his father what he heard in this room? Jason was determined to find out.

The next day began like many others. Dele-

gates filed into the stuffy room. They smiled at Jason, their dutiful water boy. His cool water, as always, would be most appreciated.

Jason listened to the soft-spoken James Madison as a pupil listened to a teacher. He admired Madison's tireless patience. He answered every question that the delegates had about his plan. Now Jason wanted his question answered.

Jason sighed in disgust. The words he heard were familiar, but they still meant nothing to him. Then he heard something different: "a union of states," and how this "union of states" would be a land of liberty and justice for all people.

Jason smiled. "So that's what the big secret is," he thought. "The delegates aren't talking about state governments. They are talking about a new kind of government that would govern all the people!"

Jason wanted to rush out and tell his father his wonderful discovery. But he had pledged to keep what he heard at the convention a secret.

On September 17, 1787, Jason's father and the rest of the country found out Jason's secret.

Borrowing Indian Ideas

Americans owe the Iroquois people their thanks for the government we have today, as much as we do the delegates who met at the Constitutional Convention.

In 1500 many Iroquois villages were fighting each other. The Iroquois government, a loose confederacy, was unable to stop this fighting. The Iroquois leaders solved this crisis by forming a new kind of government. The villages of five Iroquois nations became the villages of one nation ruled by a council. The council consisted of members, or delegates, who represented the people. This council had the power to make decisions for all the villages.

Over 200 years later, American leaders used the principles of Iroquois government to unite the colonies, declare their independence, and form a government ruled by the people.

HARDWORKING JAMES MADISON

Each delegate who came to the convention knew the Articles of Confederation had to be changed. But few delegates had a clear idea what these changes should be.

James Madison did. He worked day and night to create a plan, the Virginia Plan. This plan was bold. It did away with the Articles of Confederation and replaced them with a strong, central government that had power over the states.

This government would have three branches. The judicial branch would have the power to evaluate laws. The executive branch would have the power to enforce laws. The legislative branch would have the power to create laws.

James Madison pushed his plan at the Constitutional Convention. He was the convention leader. Madison spoke 161 times, took notes at every meeting, and studied every night to prepare for the next day.

Most of Madison's plan was eventually included in our American Constitution. His hard work earned him the title "Father of the Constitution."

WHAT THE CONSTITUTION DID

The delegates created the Constitution, an outline for how all thirteen states would be governed. The Constitution wasn't like the Articles of Confederation. The articles had created a congress that had no power over the states. The new Constitution created a central government that made laws the states had to obey.

After the Constitution was written, each state legislature was asked to accept it. For the next six months, the states debated whether to accept the Constitution.

Eventually, nine out of thirteen states gave their approval. North Carolina voted against the Constitution. Rhode Island's legislature didn't care to vote at all. Ultimately, both states changed their opinions.

With the states' acceptance of the Constitution, the nation that we have today was created.

THE BILL OF RIGHTS

The Constitution said nothing about the people's rights. It didn't answer questions such as these: Do people have the right to worship as they like? Do people have the right to a fair trial? Do people have the right to say what they believe without being punished?

In 1791 ten amendments, or changes, were added to the Constitution. These ten amendments were called the Bill of Rights.

Every family has a set of rules they live by—even if they aren't written down. As a family, sit down and read the Bill of Rights. Develop a Family Bill of Rights. Here are some possible questions that your Family Bill of Rights could answer: Does a parent have the right to inspect your room without your permission? Is it okay for children to say anything they like to an adult? Does a parent have the right to punish a child any way he or she likes?

WASHINGTON'S DISAPPOINTMENT

George Washington had a great gift. He was able to settle arguments. He could bring people together for a common cause. It was this talent, among others, that helped him win the Revolutionary War.

When he became president, Washington chose Alexander Hamilton to be the secretary of the treasury and Thomas Jefferson to be the secretary of state. Washington admired and trusted these two young men. More than that, he thought of them as sons.

What Washington didn't know at first was that Jefferson and Hamilton despised each other. They had two opposite opinions about how the government should care for the nation. Their opposing views caused them to quarrel. President Washington could do nothing to stop them. Their differences were a great disappointment to him.

FREE IN THE NORTH, SLAVES IN THE SOUTH

Hamilton believed America's future was to become the world's greatest industrial nation. Businessmen would open factories. Jobs would be created. People would freely apply to work at the jobs of their choosing. Businessmen would make a profit. Workers would earn a living. The nation would prosper.

In the South, where Jefferson lived, farming was the main source of jobs. Most of the farms were plantations. Plantations were large farms that needed many workers to grow cash crops such as tobacco.

Southern farmers didn't hire employees to work plantations. They purchased slaves to do the work. Slave labor allowed farmers to make greater profits.

Farmers didn't have to share their profits with

James Madison's Virginia Plan divides the government into three branches: executive, judicial, and legislative. His proposal for the legislative branch caused some controversy. Madison proposed that bigger states could send more representatives to the legislature than smaller states could. The smaller states refused to accept this. Some of them, including New Jersey and Connecticut, drafted an opposing plan called the New Jersey Plan. This plan favored smaller states' rights. In what became known as the Great Compromise, two houses of the legislature were created: the Senate and the House of Representatives. Every state would have two senators, but larger states would have more representatives in the House than smaller states would.

slaves. They didn't have to pay slaves a weekly wage. Farmers gave slaves only food and a place to live.

Southern farmers were dependent on slavery to make a profit. In the North, citizens were against slavery. America was a union of states, but the issue of slavery divided this union.

WORKING TOGETHER

Despite their differences, Jefferson and Hamilton did work together. It was their teamwork that broke the deadlock in Congress over how to pay off the country's Revolutionary War debts and where the nation's capital should be located.

In exchange for the government paying the northern states' war debt, the capital would be located in the South—after remaining in Philadelphia for ten years.

Jefferson wasn't entirely pleased by this compromise. He felt he had been "made a tool for forwarding his [Hamilton's] schemes."

TWO CHILDHOODS, TWO MEN

Jefferson and Hamilton had two very different childhoods.

Jefferson was born into a wealthy farm family in Virginia. He had a tutor as a boy and became a scholar as an adult. His privileged upbringing allowed him to believe farm life was the best life an American man could have.

Hamilton was born on an island in the West Indies. He lived in poverty among fruit trees, mosquitoes, and hurricanes. At an early age, his mother snatched him away from his father to live with relatives.

When he was eleven years old, Hamilton's mother died. His relatives didn't want him. Alexander Hamilton was left on his own, with nothing but his wits to help him survive. He not only survived; he succeeded. But Hamilton never forgot his bitter childhood. It made him believe that common people were unreliable and needed to be governed by wealthy citizens.

Jefferson's and Hamilton's opinions about government were shared by many citizens. People who agreed with Hamilton were known as the Federalists, and those who agreed with Jefferson were called the Anti-Federalists. These two groups became the first two political parties in the United States of America. Which party would you belong to?

HAMILTON	JEFFERSON
I want our nation to be prosperous.	So do I.
And how do you plan to meet this goal?	Look to my home, Virginia. Men work hard. The government doesn't tell them what to do. People have prospered.
You, sir, are talking about farmers. Our nation is a country of businessmen.	Businessmen are scoundrels. They are selfish and corrupt.
How so?	Businessmen care only about profit.
As well they should. A wealthy businessman means more trade, more work, more wealth for our nation. What does a wealthy farmer mean? More land and more slaves for the farmer, but no wealth for the nation.	This nation began as farmers. It was farmers who fought and won our independence. And it will be the farmer that keeps this nation strong.
Sir, it appears your eyes can look only south, to Virginia. If you could look north, you would see people living in cities, making goods and trading with other nations.	Cities are horrible places. They destroy a man's health, his freedom, and his honor.
Cities are our future. Businessmen are our hope for the future.	And what about the people? Our Constitution begins with the words "We the people." Our government must serve the people.
The people are like unruly horses. They need someone to steer them.	And that someone is the businessman?
That is correct.	So then, the government should serve the businessmen?
That is correct. Now you understand.	I will never understand you or your beliefs.

The First Inauguration

Washington rode 260 miles to his inauguration.

Every four years, voters in America choose a new president or reelect the one they already have. The law says the president will begin his or her job on January 20. That day is called Inauguration Day. *To inaugurate* means to begin. The new president's first day of work begins with ceremony and celebration. At noon on that day, the president takes the oath of office, a vow to do the best job possible.

In the evening there are large parties and dances to honor the new president. Dressed in formal clothes, the president visits as many of these as possible, to thank everyone who helped him win the election.

Some inaugural traditions began in 1783. Others have been added as times and ideas have changed.

On February 4, 1789, George Washington was chosen the president by sixty-nine electors who met in New York City. The electors chose him unanimously—that means he got every vote—and then they voted for a vice president. John Adams got the most votes, so he would serve with Washington.

Unlike presidential candidates of today, Washington didn't campaign for the job of the president. He didn't especially want to be the president. But he was by far the most popular man in America. People praised him as the general who won the Revolutionary War. After thinking long and hard about it, he decided he should put his love of the new nation ahead of his wish to retire and enjoy a quiet life in the country.

In mid-April Washington rode 260 miles from his Mount Vernon home to New York City for the inauguration. His wife Martha would arrive in May. There were no cameras or television crews, of course, but the roads were dusty with huge crowds that gathered to cheer and toss flowers in his path. At every stop there were banquets, speeches, and toasts in his honor.

Washington was a wealthy man, but for his inauguration day he wore a plain brown cloth suit made in America. Its metal buttons had eagles stamped in them, a new and unusual detail that would soon be used everywhere. He wore his best white silk stockings and black shoes, size thirteen, with silver buckles. A sword hung at his side. His hair was fixed in the style of the times—powdered white and gathered at the back of his neck.

On his inauguration day, Washington probably awoke to a booming salute by cannons. As bells rang out in celebration, he began the day by going to church. Next he watched a military pa-

HOW SHOULD
A PRESIDENT BEHAVE?

No one in America had ever been a president before, so George Washington had to make many decisions about how to do his new job. He wrote to Alexander Hamilton and John Adams. These are the issues he wanted advice on:

1. Should he seclude himself from, or avoid, the public?

2. If not, then how often should he meet the public?

3. Should he plan one day a week for visitors?

4. Should he open his office every day at 8 A.M., to meet with people who had business with him?

5. From time to time, should he have dinner with members of Congress?

6. Should he invite members of Congress to have dinner with *him*?

7. Would it be improper, or wrong, for him to visit personal friends who were not in politics?

8. Should he make a tour of the United States?

HERE'S OUR ADVICE

Alexander Hamilton thought the new president should hold one formal reception a week. The guests should come by invitation only, and the president should stay for only half an hour. Hamilton also advised Washington to appear in public only on a few national holidays. Important officials should be invited to small, private dinners. Most people should *not* be allowed to visit with the president. Presidential meetings with senators, ambassadors, and department heads were among the few Hamilton approved of. He thought the president should never be expected to return visits to those whom he invited to see him. John Adams had similar ideas for presidential etiquette, but he persuaded Washington to hold two—not one—receptions each week.

The president decided not to accept private invitations from anyone. He chose Christmas Eve, New Year's Day, and his own birthday as the three holidays when he would meet the public.

At the presidential home in New York, the Washingtons hosted many small dinners. Martha Washington, who was politely called Lady Washington, held her own receptions for friends every Friday evening.

You Write the Rules

If you were deciding how a president should behave, how would you answer George Washington's questions? Most members of Congress agreed with John Adams, who said that when Washington invited someone over, he did not necessarily have to accept an invitation back.

Here's another challenge for you. What if you were the president? Can you think of nine questions you would have about how you should act? Would you wonder if certain clothes would be okay for you to wear as the president? Would you want to be treated more like a king than an ordinary person?

Some presidents like getting out and meeting the public, but others don't. How many presidents have there been since you were born? Ask a grown-up to tell you about some of the presidents who have served in your lifetime and what they were like.

rade in his honor. At 12:30 P.M., he went to Federal Hall, where he stood on the balcony and took the oath of office. Below, a huge crowd of people gathered. As he finished the short promise to preserve, protect, and defend the Constitution of the United States, he added his own expression, "So help me God."

After taking the oath of office, he went to the Senate chamber to address the men who had elected him.

Speaking nervously sometimes, and in a low, solemn voice, President Washington spoke of the huge responsibility he faced and of his concern that he had no experience to prepare him for being the president. He thanked his fellow leaders for putting their trust in him. He told them about changes he would like in the Constitution and about how he thought they should work together. When he ended his twenty-minute talk, the cavalry escorted him to his home at No. 1 Cherry Street, New York City.

At dinner, the new president was alone for the first time that day. But soon a horse-drawn carriage came to pick him up for the fireworks. All over New York, candles were lighted in windows. In public parks and private yards, citizens lit lanterns and flares in a great celebration for the new leader and the new nation.

America's "First Granddaughter"

They stopped along the way to watch parades.

"Miss Eleanor Custis . . . has more perfection . . . than I have ever seen before." This flattering remark was made about George Washington's step-granddaughter, "Nelly." She was a beautiful and intelligent girl who, with her brother, George Washington Parke Custis, was raised by the president and Mrs. Washington.

The children's father had died after the battle of Yorktown ended the Revolutionary War. Nelly was two and "Wash" was a baby when George and Martha agreed to raise them. Their older sisters stayed with their mother.

Nelly was ten when President Washington took her to New York to live. They stopped along the way to watch parades and to smile at the people sitting on fences or crowding the roadside. Pretty little Nelly felt "carriage sick" during the long, bumpy ride.

In 1789 New York was the temporary capital of the new nation and a center for art, music, and fashion. The Washingtons got a tutor for Nelly, who gave her private lessons in painting and music. She also went to an academy where she learned geography, grammar, French, embroidery, and dancing.

Nelly dearly loved her "Grandpapa" and "Grandmama," and many of the president's hobbies, such as gardening, became hers. One day she said she hoped to become a great farmer like him.

When Washington finally retired, the family went home to Mount Vernon. Nelly loved the country. "I never have a dull or lonesome hour, never find a day too long," she told a friend.

THE CABINET GAME

Have you ever wanted to raise your allowance or wished that someone else would write your thank-you notes for you? Become the president and turn your family members or a few friends into your "cabinet" and let them help you with your work.

Ask five friends or family members to play the Cabinet Game with you. You might want to dress up in old-fashioned hats and suits.

How You Play:

On separate slips of paper, write the titles of your five cabinet members, fold them up, and put them in a dish. The titles are: secretary of war, chief justice, secretary of state, secretary of the treasury, and attorney general. Let each person choose one.

Think of four or five problems or tasks you want help with. These things will be your "agenda," the things you hope to accomplish as a cabinet. Try to include a situation from each of these areas: getting along with friends or siblings (secretary of war), raising your allowance or buying something (secretary of the treasury), and writing a letter to someone, finishing a project, or inviting a friend over (secretary of state). Every cabinet member can help you decide on the agenda, but the attorney general and you should make the final decision.

Ask the secretary of state to write down the agenda. Begin the cabinet meeting by reading the agenda and setting a time limit for each item.

Listen to every opinion and suggestion, especially from the secretary who will then complete the task. (If you decide to rent a movie, for example, the secretary of the treasury should find the best rental price. The attorney general should make sure the movie's rating is acceptable to everyone's family rules. If you want to have a sleepover, the secretary of state should call the parents and get permission.)

Your cabinet may find it disagrees on some things or the secretary doesn't want to do what is decided. In that case, the chief justice steps in to listen and advise, too. He or she should help solve disagreements, remind everyone to take turns, and keep an eye on the time.

When you finish the game, talk about what you accomplished, what didn't work, and why. When you're ready, play the game again, choosing different roles and with a new agenda to work on.

President Washington chose a small group of trustworthy men to help him decide how the government should be run. His advisors were named to head important departments. They met privately, in a small meeting room sometimes called a cabin. From that word we get the expression, the "President's cabinet." Washington selected five cabinet members; today there are thirteen, chosen by the president and confirmed, or approved, by Congress.

Washington chose Henry Knox as the secretary of war, to make national military decisions. He named John Jay as the chief justice of the Supreme Court. Thomas Jefferson became the secretary of state, to handle business with foreign nations; Alexander Hamilton was appointed secretary of the treasury, to make decisions about the nation's budget and money supply; and Washington's young friend Edmund Randolph became the attorney general, whose job it was to give the president legal advice.

Listen to every opinion and suggestion.

Benjamin Banneker Surveys the Capital

Banneker didn't know when he would return.

On a cold morning in February 1791, Benjamin Banneker swung his stout body up onto his horse. He was dressed neatly in a long waistcoat and trousers. Under his broad-brimmed hat, his hair stood thick and white against his dark skin. His clothes and scientific journals were in a pack behind his saddle. He did not know when he would return. His sisters had promised to look after his farm.

Banneker had fretted about what to take to Virginia. In his sixty years, the black man had never spent a single night away from the little cabin on his Maryland farm. He was muscular from years of hard work, but he was unaccustomed to long trips on horseback. His joints would ache during the ride. But he would make the best of it, for he was about to experience the greatest adventure of his life.

He followed the road through the valley to George Ellicott's store, where Major Andrew Ellicott was waiting for him. President Washington had appointed the major to survey a ten-mile square along the Potomac River for the new federal territory. The major lived in Phila-

delphia. He had recently surveyed the western boundary of New York. His cousin George had told him about Banneker, who had taught himself mathematics and astronomy.

Banneker lived alone, but he was welcome among his prosperous Quaker neighbors. He often went to the Ellicott store to buy paper, ink, molasses, and other goods. He sometimes stayed to read the newspaper that arrived from Baltimore. Most of all, he enjoyed discussing science with his friend George Ellicott. It was George who thought Banneker would make a good assistant on Andrew's mapping project.

On February 7, Banneker and Ellicott arrived in Alexandria, Virginia. While they waited for bad weather to clear, they set up the surveyor's tent that would hold their supplies. Andrew Ellicott owned the finest astronomical instruments in America. He put Banneker in charge of them. Banneker slept on a cot in the tent.

Ellicott hired woodcutters to clear roads. He organized the engineering camp at the top of a hill. He felled a tree and set his astronomical clock on the stump. The main tent, with a flap in the roof, was set up around the stump. One of the instruments in the tent—a zenith sector—pointed through the flap toward the sky.

Looking through the zenith sector at night, an observer could see the stars directly overhead as they crossed the meridian, an imaginary line that runs through the North and South Poles. Recording the time and averaging the distances between these stars as they crossed the sky, the astronomer could calculate the latitude. Using a telescope to study the time of certain eclipses on Jupiter, he could figure out the land's longitude.

As Ellicott's assistant, Benjamin Banneker recorded the exact time of the stars' movements every night. He had to keep the astronomical clock precise. He kept it wound and made sure it stayed at a fairly constant temperature. To be sure it kept exact time, he measured its time against the movement of the sun during the day.

While Ellicott was surveying, Banneker took care of the instruments. He sometimes went with Ellicott to meetings. From evening until

From evening until dawn Banneker did the sky work.

dawn he did the sky work. He fell asleep at sunrise, only to be awakened early, when Ellicott arrived to begin his day's work. The men went over their charts and talked about the survey's progress.

During the day, as Banneker tried to rest, workmen came and went inside the tent. The older man had never slept in a tent before. Some nights were very cold. But he understood the importance of the work, and he accepted the discomforts. He was pleased to be learning so much.

Americans were interested in the work of laying out the federal territory and building the capitol. A newspaper account from Georgetown, Virginia, reported: "Some time last month arrived in this town Mr. *Andrew Ellicott*, a gentleman of superior astronomical abilities. He was employed by the President of the United States of America, to lay off a tract of land, ten miles square, on the Potomac, for the use of Congress;—is now engaged in this business, and hopes soon to accomplish the object of his mission. He is attended by *Benjamin Banniker*,

Banneker's Family History

Misfortune brought Banneker's grandmother, Molly Welsh, to America from England. She had been accused, perhaps wrongly, of stealing a pail of milk from the dairy farm where she worked. In America she was sold to a tobacco farmer. When she completed her seven-year indenturement, or term of service, she received fifty acres of land.

Molly needed help clearing her land. She bought two male slaves. One, Bannka, was the son of an African chief. When her farm became successful, she gave the slaves their freedom. Then she married Bannka.

Molly and Bannka's oldest daughter, Mary, married a former slave named Robert, who had become a Christian. Because he had no last name, they kept Mary's name, by now spelled "Bannecky."

The Banneckys were Benjamin's parents. They took him to church and sent him to school. They saved their money and bought more land. When Robert signed the deed of sale, he put Benjamin's name on it, too. When his father died, Benjamin inherited the land.

an Ethiopian, who . . . [has proven] abilities as a surveyor, and an astronomer."

In the little free time Banneker had, he worked on his own project. He was making calculations for an almanac, a calendar that tells the times of sunrise and sunset, tides, phases of the moon, and eclipses. He hoped to find a printer who would publish and sell it when it was finished.

As the weather improved, mapping went faster. By April, the ten-mile area was measured and boundary lines were laid. President Washington met with Ellicott to see the survey map and then visited the grounds in person.

On April 15, 1791, a ceremony was held in Alexandria to place a stone marker to honor the site where the survey began. It was an exciting day for the new nation. Ellicott, Banneker, the mayor of Alexandria, and other dignitaries attended. Ellicott measured the spot for the marker. It was lowered into place with instruments that held special meaning for the district where democracy would soon rule. So the marker would not be placed lopsided, a carpenter's level was used, as a symbol of equality. It was adjusted with a T square, for virtue, and a plumb line, which measures a straight vertical

line, for moral uprightness. When the stone was set, it was dedicated with rituals borrowed from other cultures. Wine and oil were poured over the marker, as symbols of joy and peace. Corn, a symbol of nourishment and goodness, was sprinkled over it as well.

The first phase of surveying was completed. Benjamin Banneker had done his part. He was reluctant to see his work with Major Ellicott end, but he went home with pride in his accomplishments. Now he could finish his almanac.

A DAY WITH A SCIENTIST

If you had lived near Benjamin Banneker, in Baltimore County, Maryland, in the 1790s, you probably would have agreed that he was a good neighbor. With his fine manners and kind speech, he made visitors feel welcome. He earned a living from the tobacco he grew and sold, but he had a burning interest in scientific things. You would have been surprised at the activity that went on in and around his cabin on the hill.

Banneker owned 125 acres of rolling farmland and woods near the Patapsco River. With horses to ride, a small orchard of fruit trees, and a creek that ran through the valley below his

Banneker's Almanac

Banneker's first almanac, for 1791, was printed in Philadelphia and Baltimore, two of the largest cities in America. The printer in Philadelphia was a Quaker who believed slavery was wrong. He knew many people would want to see the scientific work of a free black man.

Banneker's first almanac was a big success. He published another every year until his health worsened in 1797.

Banneker sent his first almanac with a letter to Thomas Jefferson, who had written in the Declaration of Independence that "all men are created equal." He asked Jefferson to enlarge his heart with kindness and help stop the cruelty to "my brethren in captivity." Jefferson answered that he deeply wished to see a good system begin to help slaves. Both letters were printed in Banneker's almanac for 1792.

He might teach you the names of the constellations.

Benjamin Banneker

cabin, it would have been a great place to play. In the summer you could pick ripe pears from the old tree beside his house or hunt for blackberries in the thorny thicket near the road.

You could go exploring. You might disappear for a while among the tall rows of tobacco plants in the fields. You could hike to the top of a hill to enjoy a view of the countryside and then roll back down to the creek that rippled its way to the river. You could go for a cool swim and maybe catch a few frogs or turtles.

Inside Banneker's dark little cabin there was plenty to do, too. The silence there was broken only by the steady ticking of the wooden clock Banneker had designed and built. You might have played his violin and flute.

If you were having trouble with your math or science homework, Banneker would have been just the one to help you. Or you could help him make drawings for his almanac. You would have worked at the big table his neighbor gave him, writing by candlelight the way he always did.

The best part of the day at Banneker's house might be the evening, when you would understand why he is called America's first black scientist. He would teach you how to calculate when the full moon would rise and when to expect an eclipse. On the table in front of the window, you would set up the pedestal telescope his neighbor had loaned him. While you peered through the telescope at the night sky, your friend might teach you the names of the constellations. Then you would go outside and see how many stars you could identify with the naked eye.

By then it might be too late to walk home, so Benjamin Banneker might invite you to spend the night. You would climb the ladder to the cabin's small loft and fall asleep on a mattress filled with chicken feathers.

A PERMANENT CAPITAL

George Washington took the oath of office in 1789 in New York City. As the largest city in the United States, it became the nation's temporary capital. But almost at once Congress passed a bill that would move the capital back to Philadelphia, where it had been before and during most of the Revolution. Thanks to the hard work of southern leaders, the bill also said that within ten years, or by 1800, a grand "Federal City" would be built on the banks of the Potomac River.

Work on the new capital began almost at once but would take many years to complete. In 1793, when Washington was unanimously elected again, he took the oath of office in Philadelphia. John Adams, the second president of the United States, was also sworn in at Philadelphia. But he left Philadelphia in 1798 to move into the unfinished President's House in the city of Washington, as it was now called. Mrs. Adams washed and hung out her laundry in an unfinished room that later became the East Room. The new residents had no bodyguards and no security system. Anyone could wander onto the grounds of the President's House. Nearby, hunters found plenty of deer, grouse, and wolves to shoot within the city limits.

In 1801 Thomas Jefferson took the oath of office in Washington, D.C. He made many changes to the President's House, including building its first indoor bathrooms.

The famous house earned the popular name we know today when James and Dolley Madison moved in. They filled the house with beautiful new furnishings and china, and President Madison had the house painted. With Madison, the President's House became the White House.

Work began almost at once.

A Trip with Father

The Louisiana Territory was bought and sold a number of times before the United States purchased it. In 1763 Spain bought the Louisiana Territory from France. In 1800 Spain sold the territory back to France, who eventually sold it to the United States.

Seven-year-old Thomas Jefferson, red-haired and freckled, grabbed his pack and raced outside. He didn't want to miss a minute of the adventure. He was going with his father into the Virginia wilderness to survey land.

Thomas watched his father lift a heavy pack onto a horse's back. Thomas had always admired his father's strength. He'd never forgotten seeing his father once lift a 1,000-pound barrel of tobacco from its side to a standing position.

His father mounted his horse. Thomas, who was tall for his age, was proud to be able to mount his horse all by himself. He followed his father's lead.

Thomas and his father traveled through dense forests of towering trees. His father told Thomas the trees' names and the best way to cut them down. He showed him how to cross swift mountain streams. His father laughed when a fish jumped from the water into his son's lap.

Thomas's father stopped his horse before a marked tree. He looked at his map and said, "Thomas, bring your horse beside me."

His father showed him how to read the map; then they dismounted. Thomas's father spent the afternoon instructing him how to use survey equipment. When the survey was completed, they set up camp.

That night, as bears and mountain lions prowled beyond the shadows of their campfire, Thomas listened to his father's stories about the wilderness. He told Thomas about meeting Indians. His father didn't speak of fighting; he told young Thomas about Indian customs and the peaceful conversations he had had.

Even when Thomas and his father lay down to sleep, their conversation continued. Thomas fell asleep as his father talked about the stars. The next day, they headed home.

Thomas's father spent the afternoon teaching Tom to survey.

Thomas and his father went out other times to survey land. On each occasion, Thomas learned more. His time with his father wasn't just an adventure. It was an education. Thomas learned so much. Most important, he learned a love for the land.

When Thomas was fourteen, his father died, and Thomas became the head of the family. He was young, but he was able. His father had taught him to read, to write, to survey land, and how to manage a plantation. Thomas had faith in his father's teachings and in the land.

THE LOUISIANA PURCHASE

In 1801 Thomas Jefferson became the third president of the United States. Though he was the president, his love for farm life was just as strong as when he was a boy.

He was sickened by city life, with its overcrowding and its dirty streets. The city wasn't the place citizens should live. What people needed, thought Jefferson, was the opportunity of new territory to farm. America needed more land.

President Jefferson purchased the Louisiana Territory from the French government for $15 million. This vast territory stretched south to the Gulf of Mexico and west of the Mississippi River to the Rocky Mountains. The Louisiana

Purchase doubled the size of the United States. Americans now had an extra 830,000 square miles of land to farm.

This land, however, wasn't uninhabited. Indian people were living on the land before there was a United States or even before the thirteen colonies were founded.

President Jefferson wanted Indians to become American farmers, go to American schools, and live under American laws. He believed that just as farming was the best way of life for Americans, it had to be the best way of life for Indians, too.

The Indian people loved the land as much as President Jefferson did. But they didn't need to become American farmers to prove it.

Jefferson Couldn't Wait

The Constitution didn't give Congress the right to purchase property such as the Louisiana Territory. In order for the Louisiana Territory to be purchased legally, the Constitution would need to be amended, or changed. That would take time.

During the delay, anything could happen. Congress might decide to oppose the purchase. The French might withdraw their offer to sell the Louisiana Territory.

President Jefferson couldn't risk waiting until the Constitution was amended. Even though he had no authority, he purchased the Louisiana Territory for the good of the country.

One Step from Death

Ninety feet below, the waters roared.

Captain Meriwether Lewis stood still, waiting for his heart to stop pounding. Cautiously, he started along the slippery ledge. Drawn by a deadly fascination, he looked down through the cool shadows of the pine trees. Ninety feet below, the waters of the Missouri River roared. Crashing over a bed of rocks, the river tumbled angrily through the canyon. Lewis turned his head, seeing the fresh streak of mud caked on his pant leg from his fall. It had been a close call. Only his spear had saved him from plunging over the bluff to his death.

Suddenly a cry of terror pierced the air.

"Captain! Captain! What shall I do!"

Lewis recognized Richard Windsor's voice. Lewis turned cautiously, so he wouldn't slip again. He was sickened by the sight that greeted him. Windsor, too, had lost his footing on the muddy path. He lay on his belly. The right side of his body hung over the ledge. In desperation Windsor dug his fingers into the clay. He tried to wedge the tip of his left foot into the earth.

Captain Lewis's stomach lurched. Needles of sweat shot across his forehead. Any minute, Windsor might lose his grip and vanish over the edge. Lewis was too far ahead of the young soldier to reach him in time. Even if he could, the bluff above the river was too narrow for both of them.

Lewis hid his terror. He took a deep breath. He made his voice level.

"Stay calm. You're in no immediate danger. Don't answer me. Just listen, and do as I direct."

The crisis demanded swift thinking. Lewis spotted the long knife in Windsor's belt.

"Reach behind you—slowly—with your right hand, and draw your knife," he ordered. He watched as Windsor gingerly pulled the sharp blade from its sheath.

"Good. Now carefully reach below the bank and dig a cavity for your foot."

Lewis watched as Windsor followed his instructions. Seconds passed like hours. Globs of mud dropped away from the blade. If luck failed, the man would lose his balance and vanish. But Windsor held his body taut, controlling every muscle. Inch by inch, his toe found its way toward the wide hole he had carved. Slowly, he anchored his foot securely into the ledge. When he felt steady, he raised himself to his knees.

"You're almost there," Lewis encouraged. But then he saw the mud caked on the soles of Windsor's feet. "Slip out of your moccasins and let them drop," he instructed. "Then come forward along the bluff."

Relief flooded over Lewis as he watched Windsor, gun in one hand and knife in the other, crawl to a spot wide enough for him to stand.

Once again, the men of the Lewis and Clark expedition had risked danger and survived. But within minutes, two men had faced death on this ledge. That was too risky.

Lewis called to the men who followed. He ordered them to retreat down the bluff and cross the river where it was only chest deep. On the opposite bank, they would wade through the mud. Where the river was over their heads, they would cut footsteps in the bank and climb beside the water.

That night the men sat in the shelter of an abandoned Indian camp. They ate a freshly killed deer. Rain drizzled down between the branches. Lewis sat alone as he often did, enjoying the solitude. He needed to think constantly about the safety and well-being of every man in his party. They had come 2,220 miles in thirteen months. It was still 1,000 miles to the Pacific Ocean. Meriwether Lewis could not relax yet.

Lewis ordered the men to cross the river.

THE LEWIS AND CLARK EXPEDITION

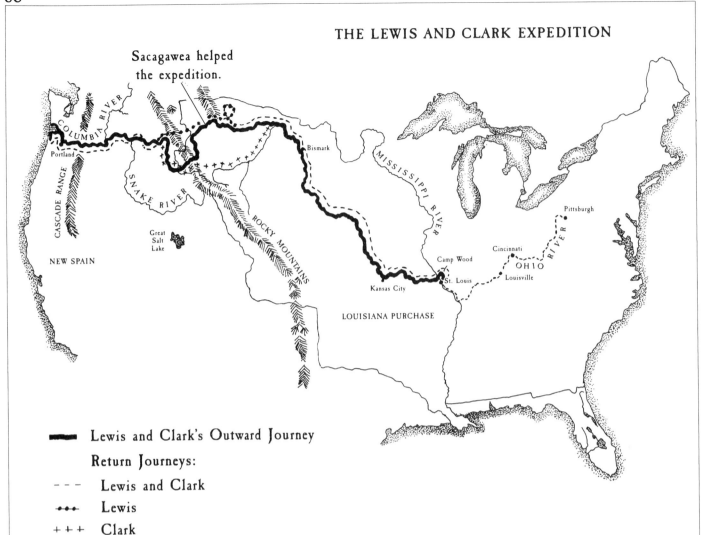

Sacagawea helped the expedition.

COLUMBIA RIVER

Portland

CASCADE RANGE

SNAKE RIVER

Great Salt Lake

NEW SPAIN

ROCKY MOUNTAINS

Bismark

MISSISSIPPI RIVER

Pittsburgh

Cincinnati

OHIO RIVER

Camp Wood

St. Louis

Louisville

Kansas City

LOUISIANA PURCHASE

——— Lewis and Clark's Outward Journey

Return Journeys:

- - - Lewis and Clark

•••• Lewis

+ + + Clark

Meriwether Lewis

William Clark

In 1804 Meriwether Lewis and William Clark set out across the continent, with a "shopping list" of all the things President Jefferson hoped they would see, learn about, or collect and bring back. This map shows their route. They followed the Missouri River to the Rocky Mountains. There they faced their biggest danger. They needed to cross the Rockies before severe winter snowstorms blocked the passes, but the men had no horses. Without the help of their Indian friend, Sacagawea, the expedition was doomed at the Continental Divide. As they reached the mountains, the Shoshone woman discovered the

Indian tribe of her childhood. Even more surprising, her brother had become the chief. The friendly Shoshone sold the soldiers enough pack horses to safely cross the mountains. Sacagawea, her newborn baby, and her husband accompanied Lewis and Clark on the rest of the journey. Safely over the Rockies, the expedition followed the canyons, rapids, and falls of the Salmon, Snake, and Columbia Rivers. On November 7, 1805, William Clark wrote in his journal, "Great joy in camp we are in view of the Ocian, this great Pacific Octean which we [have] been so long anxious to See."

Lewis and Clark held many meetings on their way from the Missouri River to the Pacific Ocean. Here Lewis addresses Oto and Missouri Indians at what came to be known as Council Bluffs on August 3, 1804.

A Historic Journey

The Lewis and Clark expedition, called the "Corps of Discovery," explored 7,000 miles of United States territory. In 1803 a journey such as this one, across unknown territory, was extremely dangerous. The expedition remains one of the greatest feats in American history.

Thirty soldiers, some Indian interpreters, and a black servant made up the exploration party. Led by Meriwether Lewis and William Clark, they left St. Louis on May 14, 1804. Rowing north up the Missouri River, they filled three rowboats. The men who wrote to their families at the start of the journey knew they might never get home again.

Lewis and Clark were an unusual team. They had fought together in the Revolutionary War and remained friends. Many years later, Lewis became private secretary to President Thomas Jefferson. When Jefferson chose him to lead the expedition, Lewis wanted Clark to accompany him. The government hired Clark as a second lieutenant, but Lewis insisted that he be called "captain." They were partners in making decisions.

Jefferson wanted Lewis and Clark to map the land that the United States had just bought from the French emperor. The president persuaded Congress to spend $2,500 on the scientific trip, which lasted over two years. In addition to their map making, Jefferson expected them to gather samples of plants, animals, fish, fossils, and Indian artifacts.

When they returned in 1806, Lewis and Clark were famous. Scientists, other explorers, and ordinary people waited eagerly to learn what the explorers had discovered. The expedition provided knowledge that made it easier for others to continue exploring the West. Yet it also threatened the hunting grounds and lifeways of Indians who had lived on the land for centuries.

When the expedition ended, some of the explorers published books based on their journals, maps, and drawings. Here are some passages from Lewis's writings:

July 4, 1804. "The morning of the 4th [of] July was announced by the discharge of our

The boats of the Corps of Discovery were no match for the wild rivers of the West. Accidents like this were common but never fatal.

gun. . . . One of our men was bitten by a snake, but a poultice of bark and gunpowder was sufficient to cure the wound. . . . To this creek which had no name, we gave that of Fourth of July creek; above it is a high mound, where three Indian paths centre. . . . After fifteen miles sail we came to . . . a creek on the southern side, about thirty yards wide, which we called Independence creek, in honour of the day, which we could celebrate only by an evening gun, and an additional gill of whiskey to the men."

July 18, 1804. "We passed several bad sandbars in the course of the day, and made eighteen miles, and encamped on the south, opposite to the lower point of the Oven islands. The country around is generally divided into prairies, with little timber . . . and near creeks, and that consisting of cottonwood, mulberry, elm, and sycamore. The river falls fast. An Indian dog came to the bank; he appears to have been lost and was nearly starved: we gave him some food, but he would not follow us."

Undated (July 1804). "We [camped] here several days, during which we dried our provisions, made new oars, and prepared our [reports] and maps of the country we had passed, for the president of the United States. . . . The present season is that in which the Indians go out into the prairies to hunt the buffaloe; but as we discovered some hunter's tracks, and observed the plains on fire in the direction of their villages, we hoped that they might have re-

turned to gather the green Indian corn. . . . [We] despatched two men to the Ottoes or Pawnee villages with a present of tobacco, and an invitation to the chiefs to visit us. . . . They found no Indians there, though they saw some fresh tracks of a small party."

July 31, 1804. "We waited with much anxiety [for] the return of our messenger to the Ottoes. . . . Our apprehensions were at length relieved by the arrival of a party of about fourteen Ottoe and Missouri Indians, who came at sunset, on the second of August, accompanied by a Frenchman, who resided among them, and interpreted for us. Captains Lewis and Clarke went out to meet them, and told them that we would hold a council in the morning. In the mean time we sent them some roasted meat, pork, flour, and meal; in return for which they made us a present of watermelons."

August 3, 1804. "The next morning the Indians . . . were all assembled . . . [and] paraded for the occasion. A speech was then made, announcing to them the change in the government, our promises of protection, and advice to their future conduct. . . . We then proceeded to distribute our presents. . . . To the six chiefs who were present, we gave a medal, ... paint, garters, . . . a cannister of powder, a bottle of whiskey, and a few presents to [everyone], which appeared to make them perfectly satisfied. The airgun too was fired, and astonished them greatly. . . . The incidents just related, [prompted] us to give to this place the name of

Soldiers constructing one of the forts that Lewis and Clark built on their journey. This one may be Fort Mandan in North Dakota.

the Council-bluff; the situation of it is . . . favorable for a fort and trading factory. . . . The ceremonies of the council being concluded, we set sail in the afternoon, and encamped at the distance of five miles, . . . where we found the mosquitoes very troublesome."

May 5, 1805. "The wolves are also very abundant, and are of two species. First, the small wolf . . . of the prairies, which are found in almost all the open plains. . . .

"Captain Clarke and one of the hunters met this evening the largest brown bear we have ever seen. As they fired, he did not attempt to attack, but fled with a most tremendous roar, . . . although he had five [musket] balls passed through his lungs and five other wounds, he swam more than half across the river to a sandbar, and survived twenty minutes. He weighed between five and six hundred pounds at least, and measured eight feet seven inches and a half from the nose to the . . . hind feet."

May 9, 1805. "The game is now in great quantities, particularly the elk and buffaloe, which last is so gentle that the men are obliged to drive them out of the way with sticks and stones."

August 15, 1805. "The [Jefferson] river is as it has been for some days shallow and rapid; and our men, who are for hours together on the river, suffer not only from fatigue, but from the extreme coldness of the water, the temperature of which is as low as that of the freshest springs in our country. In walking along the side of the river, captain Clarke was very near being bitten twice by rattlesnakes, and the Indian woman [Sacagawea] narrowly escaped the same misfortune."

November 7, 1805. "At a distance of twenty miles from our camp we halted at a village of Wahkiaeums, consisting of seven ill-looking houses. . . . We merely stopped to purchase some food and two beaver skins, and then proceeded. . . . We had not gone far from this village when the fog cleared off, and we enjoyed the delightful prospect of the [Pacific] ocean; that ocean, the object of all our labours, the reward of all our anxieties. This cheering view exhilirated the spirits of all our party, who were still more delighted on hearing the distant roar of the breakers. We went on with great cheerfulness under the high mountainous country which continued along the right bank, . . . having made during the day thirty-four miles, we spread our mats on the ground, and passed the night in the rain."

Men of the Corps of Discovery standing at the mouth of the Columbia River viewing the Pacific Ocean for the first time.

FLANNEL SHIRTS AND PORTABLE SOUP

The Lewis and Clark expedition succeeded in part because Lewis and Clark were strong leaders. But their strong friendship and respect for each other was just as important, helping them handle difficult times. Even when they struggled through the hardest days, they encouraged their men to keep going.

President Jefferson's planning added to the success of their trip, too. He cautioned them to avoid danger by putting safety first. He also asked a famous Philadelphia doctor, Benjamin Rush, to advise them about good health, disease, medicine, and treatments to use if anyone suffered on the journey.

Some of the advice Dr. Rush gave makes sense now, too. He taught them the importance of staying warm (by wearing flannel undershirts), getting enough rest, and eating lightly. He emphasized the importance of cleanliness and fresh air. His advice for wearing moccasins and taking care of cold feet worked. Not a single man lost a toe to frostbite.

To fight fevers, Lewis and Clark took along a special bark grown in Peru, which worked like aspirin. An important part of the expedition diet was something called "portable soup." It was made ahead of time by cooking beef, veal, and mutton slowly until the meat fell off the bones, then adding egg whites to make a thick paste that could be cut into squares and dried.

The expedition took nearly 200 pounds of this dried soup on the journey. The men mixed it with water or melted snow. This portable soup saved their lives on the return trip through the Rockies, when other food was scarce.

The Capitol Is Burning

"Save that picture," she ordered.

Over 4,000 enemy British troops were stationed sixteen miles from the capital of the United States! A fleet of enemy warships was anchored in Chesapeake Bay. It was war, the War of 1812.

European ships stopped American trade ships from reaching Europe. American ships were seized and their sailors were imprisoned. The United States needed to trade with Europe to be prosperous. Americans were fed up. They called on President Madison, the fourth president of the United States, to declare war on Great Britain.

For the past two years, British and American forces had waged war, mainly in Canada. Men had died. Neither side was winning. Now, in 1814, the war was approaching the American capital!

The British were in Bladensburg, the last town before the capital. The president, his advisors, and 3,000 men hurried to challenge the advancing enemy. In the capital, at the President's House, Paul Jennings went about his duties. In the near 100-degree heat, the young servant prepared the dining room for a banquet dinner. President Madison told him to expect forty guests, including his advisors and a few military gentlemen.

The boy set the table. He took out ale, cider, and Madeira, and placed the beverages in coolers.

Suddenly, he heard shouts of panic coming from outside the house. "Clear out! Clear out!" yelled Jim Smith. "General Armstrong has ordered a retreat."

The people inside were stunned. Dolley Madison, the president's wife, had hoped for victory. Now she had no choice but to run. Still, Mrs. Madison refused to go until the full-length portrait of George Washington was removed. It would be a disgrace if the painting fell into British hands.

"Save that picture," she ordered.

They Gave the British a Tough Fight

One detachment of men, led by Commodore Barney, gave the British their toughest fight at the Battle of Bladensburg. Many of the men were African Americans.

When President Madison inspected these men before the battle, he asked Barney if the "Negro" soldiers would run when the British attacked.

Said Barney, "No, sir. They don't know how to run; they will die by their guns first."

Jennings watched the doorkeeper and the gardener chop at the painting's frame until the canvas was free.

"Jennings," said Mr. Cutts, Dolley Madison's brother-in-law, "go to Fourteenth Street and fetch my carriage."

Jennings's heart pounded with fear. He left the President's House and entered a city of madness. People were running in every direction. Fleeing citizens desperately steered their wagons through dust and confusion, away from the advancing enemy.

"Go find your husband for us so we can hang him," shouted someone at Mrs. Madison. Shouts of "Hang Madison!" rang out from the street.

Jennings bravely brought the carriage back to the President's House. He watched the Cuttses leave the driveway; then he closed the door. Not long after, Jennings heard loud voices, laughter, and the sounds of objects crashing onto the floor.

Thieves were raiding the President's House! Jennings hid. When it was safe, he dashed out the door and into the twilight. Jennings headed to the ferryboat at the river.

The capital city was a ghost town. Rogues roamed the streets. Drums echoed in the night air. The British were in the nation's capital!

An American sniper fired from a building and killed the horse of British general Ross. British soldiers responded by setting the building on fire. This was how American resistance would be dealt with!

The British soldiers marched toward the Capitol Building, where the legislature met. There they heard no cries of fear, no curses. The British received a silent greeting.

The enemy stood before the Capitol. British officers Ross and Cockburn knew what to do. Their orders were unmistakable: Destroy the Capitol!

The troops—sailors and soldiers—charged up the Capitol stairs. They fired their muskets at the padlocks on the door. Cockburn led the charge into the House of Rep-

Able Men, Unable Leader

The battle at Bladensburg was an agonizing two-hour fight. August 24, 1814, was a hot day. Well-trained British forces fell dead from exhaustion because their wool uniforms caused the soldiers to become dangerously overheated.

Inexperienced American forces weren't thinking about the heat. A more terrifying problem consumed them. American forces were frightened by a new British weapon, the Congreve rocket.

The Congreve rocket was invented by Sir William Congreve. It consisted of a metal tube filled with powder and topped by a "warhead." The rocket was placed on a tripod and fired. It was rarely accurate.

That didn't matter. The deafening sound of rockets exploding was enough to send unseasoned American soldiers running for their lives.

But such horrors didn't compare to the American troops' shame at hearing the word *retreat* shouted three times in one hour by General Winder. Though the British forced the Americans to retreat, the real reason for the American defeat was that Secretary of War Armstrong had not prepared for the British attack.

People were running in every direction.

resentatives. He sat in the speaker's chair, with his men around him, and flashed a wide smile.

"Now hear this!" he roared. "Shall this harbor of Yankee democracy be burned? All in favor say aye."

"Aye! Aye! Aye!" shouted his men. Cockburn's proposal passed unanimously.

The British merrily ransacked the legislative chambers. Chairs, desks, and books were turned into kindling and heaped into huge piles. Men sprinkled the building with gunpowder and fired their rockets.

Fire raged. Windows shattered. Wind fanned the fire. The air was a swirl of heat and ashes. Nearby buildings caught on fire. The dark sky brightened from the fireball of destruction.

From the other side of the Potomac River, Paul Jennings watched President Madison and his advisors pace about, trying to decide what to do. There was nothing anyone could do. The Capitol of the United States was burning, and no one could stop it.

The Capitol was burning, and no one could stop it.

After the Fire

The New White House

The Octagon House

SAVED BY A RAINSTORM

On the afternoon of August 25, 1814, a raging storm caused torrential rain to fall over the burning capital city. The rain put out the fires and saved many buildings from being completely destroyed. Still, most governmental structures were either badly damaged or ruined.

President Madison wasted little time finding temporary dwellings for government workers in Washington, D.C. He was determined to restore the people's confidence in a government that had let enemy forces destroy their capital city. President and Mrs. Madison took up residence in the Cuttses' house, then moved a month later to Octagon House. Governmental departments were established in private houses.

Congress moved to Blodgett's Hotel. Congressmen were irritated by the stuffy small rooms. They threatened to relocate the capital city. But the city of Washington, D.C., was created specifically to be the nation's capital, and if the capital were moved, the city would die. Fearing that the capital was going to be relocated, local landowners agreed to build a brick hall near the destroyed Capitol. It was called "Brick Capitol."

During the years 1815 to 1819, governmental buildings were repaired or rebuilt. The restoration of the President's House was completed in 1818. The workmen successfully repaired the building, but they couldn't remove the burn marks on the limestone blocks made by the fire. The workmen painted the President's House, hiding the burn marks beneath coats of white paint.

Soon after, newspapers began calling the President's House the "White House." But it was no longer the house of President Madison and Mrs. Madison. In 1817 James Monroe had been elected the fifth president of the United States. President Monroe was the last of the Revolutionary War leaders to serve as the president.

In 1819 the reconstruction of the capital city was completed. President Monroe and his wife were living in the restored President's House. Congress left the "Brick Capitol" and moved into the new Capitol. Washington, D.C., the capital of our nation, was whole again—except for one minor problem. No one was sure what was the official name of President Monroe and Mrs. Monroe's home. Many called their home the "White House." Traditionalists called their home the President's House.

In 1903 President Theodore Roosevelt made the "White House" the official name. However, today books of matches used in the White House still call it the "President's House."

O say can you see ~~through~~ by the dawn's early light
what so proudly we hail'd at the twilight's last gleaming,
whose broad stripes & bright stars through the perilous fight
O'er the ramparts we watch'd, were so gallantly streaming?
And the rocket's red glare, the bomb bursting in air,
Gave proof through the night that our flag was still there,
O say does that star spangled banner yet wave
O'er the land of the free & the home of the brave?

AN INSTANT HIT

War Could Have Been Avoided!

War could have been avoided. On June 16, 1814, two days before America declared war on Britain, the British government agreed to stop tormenting American ships. Had President Madison known of this decision, he would have called off the war.

The people of Baltimore, Maryland, had wanted to battle the British for a decade. The city's large French population was quick to attack anyone who sided with the British. Now Baltimore's citizens would get their wish. The British were ready to attack the city, rich with stores of wheat and flour—not to mention a hatred for the British.

Unlike the citizens in the capital, the people of Baltimore were ready. Volunteers flowed into the city to fight. Sam Smith organized Baltimore's defense. He was calm and thorough.

When the British reached Baltimore on September 12, 1814, 16,391 volunteers waited to defend the city. A British officer realized a successful attack on the American forces was impossible. A diversion was needed to draw American forces from the city. A plan was created. The British navy would sail into Baltimore harbor. British troops would land. American forces would leave the city to defend the harbor. The British would capture Baltimore.

There was one problem with this plan. In order for this diversion to work, Fort McHenry, which protected the harbor, had to be taken by British forces. On September 13, the British launched a naval attack on the fort. The attack began at dawn.

Francis Scott Key had no choice but to watch the assault from a small vessel in the harbor. He had traveled in this boat to gain the release of an American doctor being held prisoner on a British flagship.

Key's legal skill got the doctor released. But the British admiral feared Key had overheard their attack plans, so he prevented Key and the prisoner from leaving the harbor. Key, a writer not a warrior, nervously watched British guns blast the fort. As night came, the American flag still flew above the fort's defensive wall, or rampart.

During the night, the shelling stopped. The air was filled with silence and smoke. Finally, a cannon boom broke the quiet. Key thought it was the final, and victorious, British attack on Fort McHenry. He was wrong. The shots were American cannons thwarting a British land attack. Both sides resumed their shelling. British Congreve rockets burst in the air. American and British cannons fired at each other.

At dawn, Key saw a flag sagging from its pole. He feared the worst. Then a breeze picked up the flag and displayed the Stars and Stripes. The fort had not been captured by the British. American forces had withstood the enemy attack.

Key was overwhelmed with excitement. He tried to capture his excitement in a poem. He began it on the back of a letter in his pocket. As the British retreated, he continued working on the poem at his hotel.

When he was finished, he showed the poem to enthusiastic relatives and friends. The poem was rushed to a newspaper in Baltimore, where copies were made by a young printer. Along with the copy was a note that the poem be sung to the tune of a popular drinking song.

The song was an instant hit, but the title was not. The original title, "Defence of Fort M'Henry," lasted only weeks. The new title, "The Star-Spangled Banner," will last forever.

PEACE! PEACE! PEACE!

At 4:00 P.M. on February 14, Secretary of State James Monroe and Henry Carroll, a British secretary, arrived in Washington, D.C. They brought the details of the peace treaty between America and Great Britain.

They rushed to Octagon House, President Madison's residence. Secretary Monroe couldn't contain his excitement. He was anxious to get President Madison to approve the agreement. Britain had already agreed to the terms of the treaty, but the document wouldn't be valid until President Madison and Congress gave their approval.

Secretary Monroe and Henry Carroll entered Octagon House. Upon being greeted by President Madison, they went directly upstairs. There, in a circular room, Secretary Monroe and Henry Carroll explained the details of the treaty.

The news of Secretary Monroe's arrival at Octagon House traveled quickly. Anxious congressmen, friends, and officials gathered in the drawing room at Octagon House, awaiting the president's decision. No one knew a single detail of the treaty, but everyone hoped the president would agree to sign the document.

Just after 8:00 P.M., President Madison came downstairs and told the crowd he had approved the peace treaty. "Peace!" cried Mrs. Madison. Shouts of peace were echoed by the crowd. Paul Jennings, the president's servant, picked up a fiddle and played "President's March."

Three days later, on February 17, Congress approved the peace treaty. Throughout Washington, D.C., church bells rang and rockets lit up the sky. Similar celebrations occurred throughout the country as the news of peace reached America's states.

People rejoiced. Cannons were fired. One man in Tennessee celebrated the peace treaty in a manner that gave him great satisfaction. He hung up two British uniforms named "Booty" and "Beauty." These names were supposed passwords used by British forces during the Battle of New Orleans. He picked up his rifle, aimed, and fired at the redcoat uniforms.

The news of peace even reached out to sea, where a British ship had spent months enforcing a blockade of a New England port. British sailors tossed their caps into the water and drank double rations of rum.

A Bitter War; A Happy Ending

The burning of the Capitol depressed the American spirit. But after the victory in Baltimore, Americans were confident they could win the war.

Back in London, news of the Baltimore defeat shocked the British people. There was talk of peace, not war. In Ghent, Belgium, American and British negotiators met. Neither side wanted to fight a long war. A peace treaty was signed on Christmas Eve, 1814.

But back in America, in New Orleans, no one knew a peace treaty had been signed. American general Andrew Jackson and British admiral Cochrane were poised for battle.

Two weeks after the peace treaty was signed, the Battle of New Orleans began. British forces twice tried to break Jackson's defense lines. American troops stood their ground. British spirit was low, but they tried one last all-out attack. Andrew Jackson was ready. The British assault failed. New Orleans was saved.

General Jackson was a national hero. His victory allowed Americans to forget the tragic burning of their capital city and remember that American forces won the Battle of New Orleans, the last battle of the War of 1812. A bitter war now had a happy ending.

Shouts of peace were echoed by the crowd.

The Longest Ditch in the World

It would be the longest waterway ever built.

Before the Erie Canal

The Chinese have an old saying that men should surrender to the winds and the water. It's not likely that Americans had heard this advice in 1800. When Benjamin Franklin and George Washington looked across the valleys and rivers of North America, their thoughts were not about surrender. To them, controlling the rivers meant earning profits. If waterways in the nation were somehow connected, as they were in Europe, products like wheat and furs could be shipped more quickly and cheaply than if they were hauled over rough, hilly roads.

"It's a brilliant idea!" the New Yorker exclaimed. "A canal that connects Lake Erie with the Hudson River will make New York the richest state in the union."

"It's insane," cried the elderly politician sitting across the table from him. "Such a canal would cost a fortune. President Jefferson won't give us the money."

A third man spoke up. "It's not possible to build a canal across the state," he agreed. "It'll never be completed."

A roar of voices filled the room as every man there turned to the next and threw his opinion into the debate. The New York legislators had gathered to argue about this plan to build a waterway from the Great Lakes to the Hudson River.

The idea of building a canal linking what was then called the West (the territory that is now Ohio and Michigan) to New York Harbor was not new. Long before the War of 1812, men had proposed a canal through this region as a cheap way to move people and goods across the country. For years, New Yorkers argued about it. They voted for leaders who agreed with them on the canal plan, and they voted against those who didn't.

DeWitt Clinton was a politician who tried at first to ignore the subject of the canal. For a while it worked. Five times in a row, the people elected him mayor of New York City. In an unusual move, while he was mayor they also elected him to the state senate. Later they made him governor.

As one of the state's most powerful men, Clinton could not keep avoiding the canal issue. The more he thought about this waterway, in fact, the more certain he was that it would be the greatest project ever built. As mayor, he appointed a Canal Commission to plan how it should be built. The commissioners, in turn, asked Clinton to lead them, which he agreed to do. They studied the state's geography, looking for the most direct route to Lake Erie. They hoped the route might follow rivers and lakes, with short canals built to connect the waterways where land separated them. In eastern New York, the Hudson River was wide and calm, perfect for boats carrying cargo to and from New York Harbor. But west of the Hudson, the Mohawk River was a jumble of waterfalls, rocks, and rapids—impossible to navigate. From the Mohawk, a crude wagon trail led west to Lake Ontario. Only a few miles beyond Lake Ontario lay Lake Erie, but the swift Niagara River and wide Niagara Falls created still another barrier to be avoided.

After they studied the problem thoroughly, the commissioners decided the best solution was to build a totally new waterway. It would be a canal—a man-made river—beginning at Albany, flowing beside the Hudson and the Mohawk Rivers, and then cutting west to Lake Erie. Over 300 miles long, it would be the longest waterway ever built. Canal boats—without sails or oars—would be pulled along by ropes harnessed to workhorses that clip-clopped over a gravel path beside the water.

Unfortunately for "Clinton's Ditch," as people called it, New York was not a flat state. Lake Erie was nearly 600 feet higher than the Hudson River. The lake water couldn't just flow downhill through the ditch to the Hudson. Dragging boats west against the current would be too slow, and valleys would have to be filled in to the right level.

To solve these problems, the engineers designed the canal with locks—sections where the water level could be raised or lowered. Like adjustable steps, the locks would raise or lower boats from one water level to another.

When the commissioners announced their plan, many citizens feared it would cost them millions of dollars. But Clinton was not discouraged. Day and night, he traveled the state, talking to everyone. His popularity and his enthusiasm persuaded people that he might be right about the importance of the canal.

Finally, in 1817, the state government voted to borrow money to start the project. On July 4, 1817, men drove the first stakes into the ground near the small town of Rome, New York. The

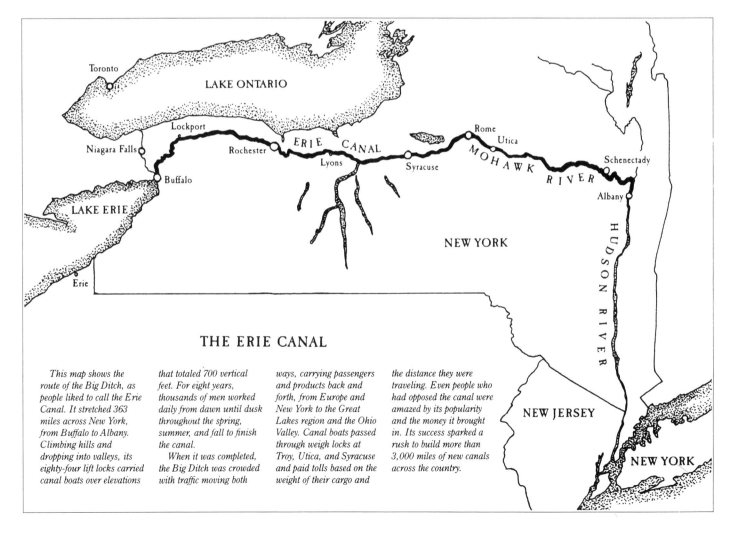

THE ERIE CANAL

This map shows the route of the Big Ditch, as people liked to call the Erie Canal. It stretched 363 miles across New York, from Buffalo to Albany. Climbing hills and dropping into valleys, its eighty-four lift locks carried canal boats over elevations that totaled 700 vertical feet. For eight years, thousands of men worked daily from dawn until dusk throughout the spring, summer, and fall to finish the canal.

When it was completed, the Big Ditch was crowded with traffic moving both ways, carrying passengers and products back and forth, from Europe and New York to the Great Lakes region and the Ohio Valley. Canal boats passed through weigh locks at Troy, Utica, and Syracuse and paid tolls based on the weight of their cargo and the distance they were traveling. Even people who had opposed the canal were amazed by its popularity and the money it brought in. Its success sparked a rush to build more than 3,000 miles of new canals across the country.

crowd cheered, cannons thundered, and Clinton—who was now the governor of New York—gave a speech. He promised the people a canal in six years.

Now the serious work began. A path 368 miles long, sixty feet wide, and twelve feet deep had to be shoveled out for the canal. Hundreds of trees, many with diameters eight or nine feet across, had to be axed down and pulled out by the roots. Swamps of oozy muck and quicksand had to be cleared and lined with walls of timber. Hillsides of rock had to be dynamited.

Men came from near and far to work for the canal-building companies. Many arrived from Ireland. They could hardly believe it was possible to make 80¢ for a single day's work! The canal crews were fed three big meals every day

and lived in a simple shack while they worked. They ate breakfast before dawn and began the workday at sunrise, not stopping until it was too dark to see. They grumbled at times, but just as often, a feeling of doing something important filled the air. For music, they called on their own talents and made up songs with silly verses.

As soon as each link in the Erie Canal was finished, it was opened for travel. In 1819 the first section was ready at Rome. It stretched only fifteen miles, but the next year a long middle section was done. Yet many New Yorkers were impatient with Governor Clinton. They nearly voted him out of office in 1820, when he announced the canal could not be finished on time.

But it *did* get finished, in October of 1825. The entire state joined in a celebration that

A parade of boats opened the festivities.

A New Canal Song

Imagine what it might have been like to work on the canal, blasting out rocks or sinking into a swamp, or to travel on a canal boat, ducking your head when you went under a low bridge overhead.

Muskrats constantly damaged the sides of the canal by burrowing into the bank. A small burrow could start a little leak, which often led to a larger land-slide along the banks. Escaping canal water caused boats to run aground in the mud. Repair crews patrolled the banks night and day, quickly patching muskrat holes with a mixture of manure and hay.

As they worked, men made up songs about their adventures and experiences on the Erie Canal. Everyone shared in the excitement of the canal, especially the travelers who piled their possessions and families on board a canal boat and headed west to start a new life. Schoolchildren all across America sang songs about the Erie, too.

We were forty miles from
*   Albany,*
*   Forget it I never shall;*
What a terrible storm we
*   had that night*
*   On the E-ri-e Canal.*

Our captain he came up on
*   deck*
*   With his spyglass in his*
*   hand.*
And the fog it was so tarnal
*   thick*
*   That he couldn't spy the*
*   land.*

Chorus:

O-o-oh the E-ri-e was a-
*   rising,*
The gin was a-getting low,
And I scarcely think
We'll get a drink
Till we get to Buffalo-o-o,
Till we get to Buffalo.

lasted for days. A parade of boats flying red, white, and blue banners opened the festivities, with Governor Clinton at the helm of the *Seneca Chief*, a fancy new boat built for the occasion. The party left Buffalo, on Lake Erie, and traveled the 523 miles to New York City. Cannons were posted every ten miles along the canal route. When the procession began, the first cannon was fired. As it thundered into the air, the next one was fired. One by one the cannons blasted the message. When the last one in New York City exploded, the signal began in reverse, rumbling back down the line toward Lake Erie.

At each stop, musicians greeted the parade of officials. Speeches praised the greatest engineering feat in American history. Sometimes dinner and dancing lasted into the night. In the morning, travelers returned to their boats and went on to the next town.

Perhaps the most unusual cargo DeWitt Clinton carried on this historic journey was two oak barrels filled with water from Lake Erie. The parade of boats took about six days to reach New York Harbor, where they were towed out to the Atlantic Ocean. Ships from around the world waited to join the celebration. Wiping back tears of joy for a dream that had finally come true, Clinton poured a barrel of Lake Erie water into the ocean. The swirling of Great Lakes water with the Atlantic symbolized the uniting of the waters of America and the world.

Stolen Freedom on the Prairie

Joseph and his father pushed their horseless cart.

Joseph Harris had heard about it. His family had heard about it. Everyone had heard about it. The Indiana Territory was the place to call home. The region had vast plains for farming and seas of wildflowers to make you smile.

People traveled to the Indiana Territory from the South. They traveled from the backcountry of Virginia and Maryland. But no matter where people came from, if they were heading westward, they all met on America's first highway, the National Road.

Never had there been such a road. The road was wide, paved with stone and gravel. Bridges spanned every stream. It was beautiful and crowded.

The National Road was a traveling circus of people, wagons, and animals. Fathers steered blanket-covered wagons bulging with bedding and supplies. Mothers walked, holding their babies. Children prodded the family pigs. Drivers urged horse teams to pull heavy freight wagons. Businessmen pranced along in fancy carriages.

In the middle of this moving madness, Joseph and his father pushed their horseless cart filled with their belongings from Baltimore, Maryland. Joseph's mother walked alongside, carrying his baby sister. It was a joyous day.

It wasn't the joy of adventure that burned in Joseph's family. It was the joy of freedom. Two months earlier, they had been a slave family in North Carolina. Now they were free because their master had died. In his will he gave them their freedom and a small amount of money. Joseph's father and mother had been slaves for twenty years.

As the sun set, the travelers camped along the roadside. Rays of sunshine gave way to rays of campfire light. Men hunted for small game. Rifle fire echoed and corn cakes sizzled.

After dinner, the sound of a fiddle, the words of a song, and conversation took over. Nearby, white boys were playing. Joseph's father wouldn't let him join in. The father had no idea how the boys' parents would react if a black boy played with their children.

Even though he was free, Joseph's father lived in fear. He knew that just as freedom allowed him to make a home on the frontier, it also allowed men who hated the color of his skin to harm his family.

When they reached Wheeling, Ohio, the Harris family purchased passage on a broad-horn flatboat. It was a huge, arklike boat. Afer several weeks on the Ohio River, the boat reached Evansville, Ohio. Joseph and his family left the boat with their cart.

The Evansville dock was buzzing with travelers and with cheats. Dishonest men sold swamp land to innocent families eager to buy. They directed travelers to lodgings, for a price.

Before the cheaters could swarm around him, Joseph's father headed to the government land office. Mr. Harris told the agent he wanted to buy land in Vincennes, fifty-five miles north of Evansville along the Wabash River.

"I've heard it's prairie land, sir," said Mr. Harris.

"That it is, but the best land has been bought up," stated the agent. "Only hundreds of cents an acre will get those who own it to part with it."

Joseph's father, like most settlers, settled for whatever land he could get. He paid the agent a dollar and was given a title for two acres of prairie land. The father walked out of the office, waving the title in the air.

After days of tough traveling, the Harris family came to Vincennes. It was a town of several hundred cabins scattered over treeless, flat land. At the western edge of the town was the Wabash River.

Joseph's father hugged his wife and children. The prairie's appearance was nothing like his slave home in North Carolina. This pleased him very much.

"This is a new land and a new life for us all," he said.

In the days that followed, Joseph and his father cut down trees from the nearby hills to build a log cabin. Neighbors joined in. Even Joseph's baby sister patted mud into the spaces between the logs for insulation.

When the cabin was finished and Joseph's mother had the inside in order, the Harris family sang hymns and feasted on salted pork and corn cakes.

That night, a group of men pushed open the cabin door. They tied up Joseph's father and took him away on horseback.

His mother screamed into the night. Joseph searched for his father's rifle. He found it, but it was too late.

Joseph never saw his father again. He was taken to a plantation and forced back into slavery. Joseph became the head of the family at age eleven. He never again went to sleep without his father's rifle beside him.

A Few Free Blacks

By 1800, America had a population of 5 million people living in sixteen states. Nine hundred thousand African Americans were slaves. America was the largest slave-holding country in the world.

But there were also free blacks in America. One out of six African Americans living in America at that time was free. Many free blacks were granted their freedom by their owners, while other blacks gained their freedom by running away. Many freed blacks resettled in northern states where slavery was outlawed.

But it was not uncommon for freed black men to be kidnapped by greedy men and returned to southern states where they were resold into slavery.

Watch Out for That Land!

Though there were large areas of fertile land on the frontier, many settlers purchased land that produced misery rather than a good life. Settlers purchased clay land that wasn't favorable for growing crops. Other land wasn't near water, or it was under water. Some streams were undrinkable. Cows ate poisonous weeds, which in turn poisoned their milk. Healthy wheat was killed by frost, blight, Hessian flies, and chinch bugs. And even land that was good for farming was often so isolated that it was difficult for families to get needed supplies or to socialize with other people.

How a Log House Was Built

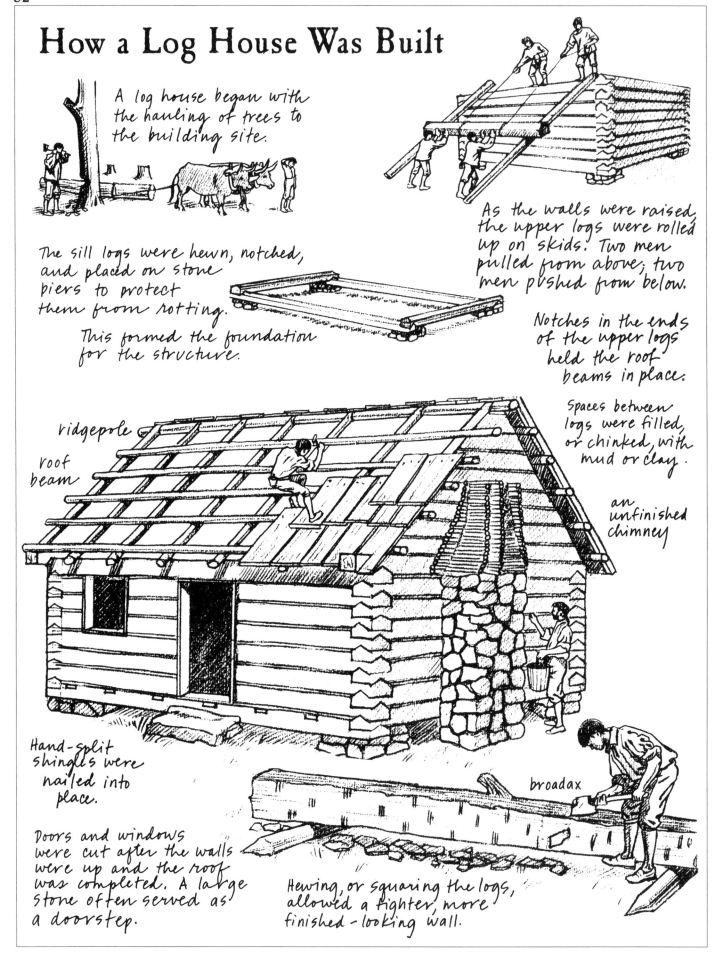

A log house began with the hauling of trees to the building site.

The sill logs were hewn, notched, and placed on stone piers to protect them from rotting.

This formed the foundation for the structure.

As the walls were raised, the upper logs were rolled up on skids. Two men pulled from above; two men pushed from below.

Notches in the ends of the upper logs held the roof beams in place.

Spaces between logs were filled, or chinked, with mud or clay.

an unfinished chimney

ridgepole

roof beam

Hand-split shingles were nailed into place.

Doors and windows were cut after the walls were up and the roof was completed. A large stone often served as a doorstep.

broadax

Hewing, or squaring the logs, allowed a tighter, more finished-looking wall.

A Frontier Town

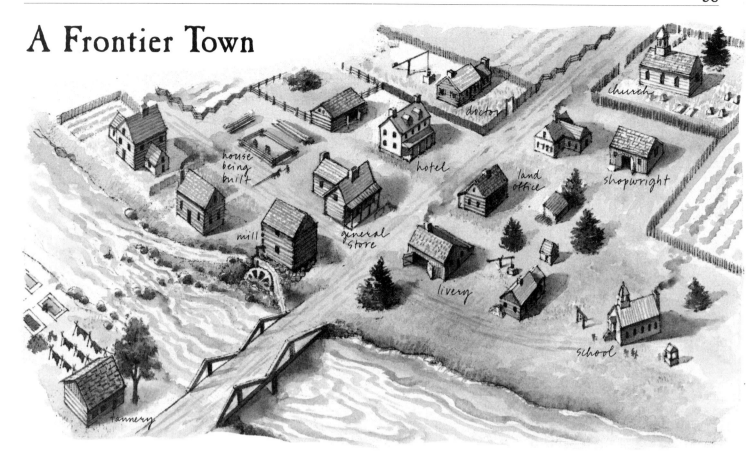

house being built

mill

general store

hotel

doctor

land office

livery

church

shopwright

school

tannery

Most frontier towns started by a river. The river allowed a frontier town to prosper. It provided a way for farmers to ship their goods to towns downriver and gave boat owners the opportunity to make a profitable living. The river offered transportation for newcomers to buy land and businessmen to make investments.

Near the water was the town's one street, Main Street. It was made of dirt and was lined with wooden structures. On Main Street a person could usually find a hotel, a general store selling everything from rope to dresses, a livery, or stable with horses, a government land office, a mill to grind wheat, and a doctor.

On and around Main Street a person could also find the town's fancy homes made of wood or brick. These homes usually had beautiful views of the river. They belonged to the families who owned the boat shipping company, the local mill, or large tracts of fertile land.

Most of the residents of a frontier town lived back from the river on one of many farmsteads scattered over the land. A farmstead consisted of several or more acres, depending on how much land a family could afford to buy. When a new family arrived in a frontier town, it was common for neighbors to gather for a house-raising. Men and boys chopped down trees.

Women and girls prepared food. Horses hauled logs back to the homesite.

The barked logs were piled into a rectangular shape about ten feet by sixteen feet in size. Where the logs crossed at the corners, the men cut a notch in the top of one log and the bottom of the other log. The logs fit together like pieces of a puzzle. The roof was made of bark or boards made from split logs. Wooden shutters, not glass, covered the windows. Women and children filled the cracks between the logs with mud and moss to keep the inside of the house dry and warm.

Frontier farmers cleared trees to plant corn and wheat. They let their pigs run wild in the woods, where they could fend for their own food. If a farmer wanted a pig, he took his rifle and went looking for one. Cows also wandered freely. Farmers, however, did keep their calves in a pen. This way the cows could be lured back to be milked.

Frontier families spent their days working the land. To the frontier farmer, Main Street was a place to get supplies, new shoes for a horse, or have wheat ground. And when it was time to take a rest from working in the field, Main Street was a place to stare at and dream of a more prosperous future.

NEITHER RAIN NOR SNOW NOR FRONTIER

By 1817, there were at least 1,000 post offices in America. If a person in New York wanted to send a letter to a friend in Vincennes, Indiana Territory, he brought his letter to the post office. The letter was folded twice, and twice again, then sealed with wax and addressed. There were no envelopes.

The letter, along with other mail, was loaded into a horse-driven cart. The driver drove the cart south on the Post Road. Along the way, he stopped at tollgates, where he paid a fee, then the gatekeeper raised the gate and let him pass. The money collected at tollgates was used to maintain the road.

Four days later the driver reached the National Road near Baltimore, Maryland. The driver traveled west on this road. His destination was Wheeling, Ohio. Again, between him and his destination were tollgates to stop him and fees to be paid.

In Wheeling the driver transferred the mail from his cart onto a flatboat or steamboat. His cart was empty, but his job wasn't over. Before leaving, he filled his cart with mail from the Wheeling post office and headed back east to New York.

Meanwhile, the mail from New York headed down the Ohio River. When the boat reached the town of Evansville, the mail was unloaded from the boat onto a cart. A driver drove the cart more than thirty miles on a poorly maintained road to the general store in Vincennes.

People went to the store to pick up their mail. Letters had no stamps, so the person picking up the mail paid the postage. The charge was based on the distance the letter traveled, not its weight. The average cost of sending a single-sheet letter was 25¢.

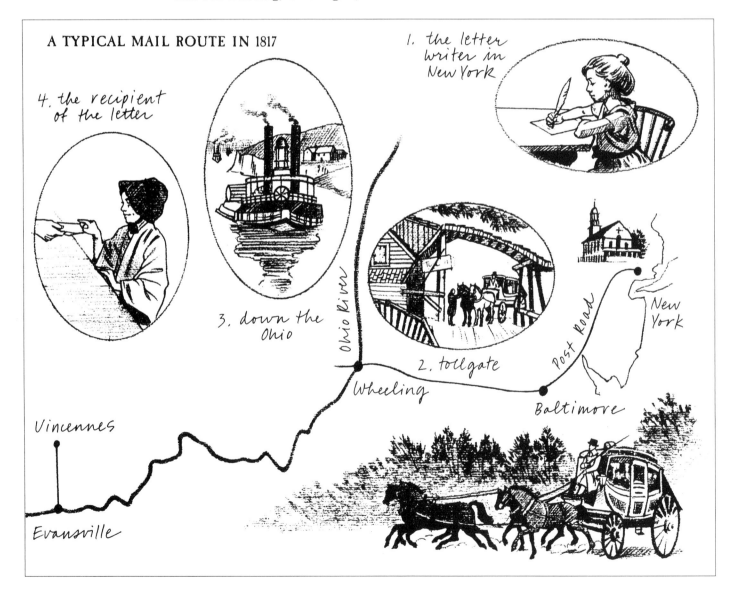

A TYPICAL MAIL ROUTE IN 1817

1. the letter writer in New York

4. the recipient of the letter

3. down the Ohio

2. tollgate

Ohio River

Post Road

New York

Wheeling

Baltimore

Vincennes

Evansville

Little School on the Prairie

Many children living on the frontier didn't attend school, for a very good reason. There were no schools! Why build a school when the children were too busy working to attend? Boys cleared and plowed the land and hunted deer and wild pigs. Girls spun wool, made clothing, and cared for the younger children.

Even if a school was built, the hired teacher, or master, wasn't always qualified to teach the children. One school trustee asked a teacher, during a job interview, if the world was round or flat. He replied, "I do not know for sure, but I am prepared to teach it either way."

Not all teachers were this uninformed. There were many able teachers who performed their exhaustive duties with skill and bravery.

Frontier teachers were not only responsible for teaching students to read, write, and add; they also had to provide the books, paper, ink, and quill pens!

The schoolhouse was usually a log cabin. The desks were boards fastened beneath the windows for light. The seats were benches, and the floor was dirt.

After the teacher sat down, boys were required to remove their hats and bow. Girls had to curtsy. Students who misbehaved were whipped with sticks.

The school day was long. School began an hour after the sun rose and finished an hour before the sun set! Students brought their lunches and dinners.

In some schools, when it was time to go, the students formed a line and the teacher gave a spelling test. Those who were successful got to leave before those who were not.

What about school holidays? There was no law that children had to get a vacation from school. In the southern states, students had to play a yearly trick on their teacher to force him or her to agree to a Christmas holiday. The trick was called "turning out" the master.

One day, near Christmas, the bigger boys in the school asked their teacher for a week-long holiday and a treat. The teacher always refused. That night, the boys took over the school, preventing the teacher from entering. Parents sneaked inside with food and a fiddle.

The next day, the teacher pretended not to give in to the students' demands. Sometimes the teacher would storm the barricaded school and playfully swat any boy he could get his hands on. Eventually, the teacher would stop resisting and agree to a holiday. Students gathered each day at school to take part in various games. At the week's end, the teacher called, "Books!" The holiday was over. The next day, school began again.

Shuffling the Brogue

When children weren't working, the land was their amusement park. Children spent hours climbing trees and playing in creeks.

They also played organized games. One favorite game was called Shuffling the Brogue. In this game, a group of children formed a circle. In the middle of the circle stood one person who was "it." The others passed a brogue, or mitten, around the outside of the circle. The person in the middle guessed who had the brogue. If correct, the person caught with the brogue was now "it."

You can play this game, too. Find a mitten, choose who is "it," and play Shuffling the Brogue.

A Game: Do You Trust Me?

Dishonest people were waiting to take advantage of innocent travelers coming to the frontier. Would they have taken advantage of you? You'll find out when you play Do You Trust Me?

In this game, players take turns being the traveler and the person to be trusted, or not. The job of the person to be trusted is to convince the traveler you are telling the truth. The traveler's job is to listen, ask questions, and then decide if it's the truth or a lie. This game has three categories: TRAVELING, LAND, and BARGAINING.

In the TRAVELING category, the traveler can choose between flatboat or steamboat travel. The person to be trusted must convince the traveler that his or her boat is safe.

In the LAND category, the traveler is buying land. One player must convince the traveler that he or she is selling fine land.

In the BARGAINING category, the traveler is looking for lodging or is buying something at the

market. The other player sells the traveler what he wants. But is it a fair price?

To convince the traveler you are telling the truth, even if you are lying, one player must make up information cards containing facts about each category. The information can be found in this book or in books found in your library. (Ask your librarian for assistance.) The player can use any or all of the information on the card to tell the truth or to lie to the traveler.

Once these information cards are completed, you must make playing cards. You can use paper or cardboard. On each card write one of the following statements. These statements will tell you whether lying is required or whether you can tell the truth.

Your flatboat leaks, but you must have passengers.

The land is good for farming, near running water.

The hotel you recommend is dirty and

uncomfortable. **Charge 10¢ for the information.**

Charge 30¢ for fine lodging. A fair price.

Your steamboat is a fine vessel.

The bushel of wheat is 2¢ per pound, but it's full of bugs.

Charge 10¢ for a fine meal—a bargain.

Claim your flatboat can go upstream.

Charge 50¢ for a bushel of potatoes— a bargain.

The land you're selling is swampy.

The horse stable is in awful shape. You charge 75¢ a night to board a horse.

You spice up week-old meat stew. Charge 15¢ for a meal.

Land is fertile, but full of rocks and very isolated. You charge 50¢ an acre.

A bushel of potatoes is half rocks. Charge $1.

The steam engine is running poorly, but you still take passengers on your steamboat.

How to Play:

1. Decide which player will first be the traveler or the person to be trusted.

2. Shuffle the playing cards.

3. The person to be trusted picks up a card.

If the card states, for example: "The hotel you recommend is dirty and uncomfortable," you then call out, "Room for rent. Who needs a room?" If the card mentions a meal, then you can call out, "Who needs a fine meal?" Be bold. Make up sales announcements that will tempt the traveler.

4. The traveler hears the other player's announcement and says he or she is looking for whatever the other player is offering. "Yes, I am looking for land." The traveler listens and asks questions.

5. The player to be trusted asks, "Do you trust me?"

6. The traveler gives his or her answer, and the other player shows the playing card revealing if he or she was lying or telling the truth.

7. If the traveler guesses correctly, the player scores a point and continues playing. If the traveler guesses incorrectly, the two players switch roles.

8. The player who has the most correct answers, or points, is the wisest traveler and the winner.

Remember, most travelers knew very little about the boats or the territory they were moving to. They were helped and fooled by talking with other people. As the traveler, think about the kind of questions you must ask to reveal if the other player is telling the truth.

Below are six items that can be bargained for and their actual market prices in Cincinnati in 1818:

A meal: as much as 50¢

Lodging: 25¢

Horse-keeping: 75¢

Pork: 5 to 8¢ per pound

Potatoes: $1 a bushel

Wheat flour: 3 to 4¢ per pound

CLOTHING OF THE EARLY 1800S

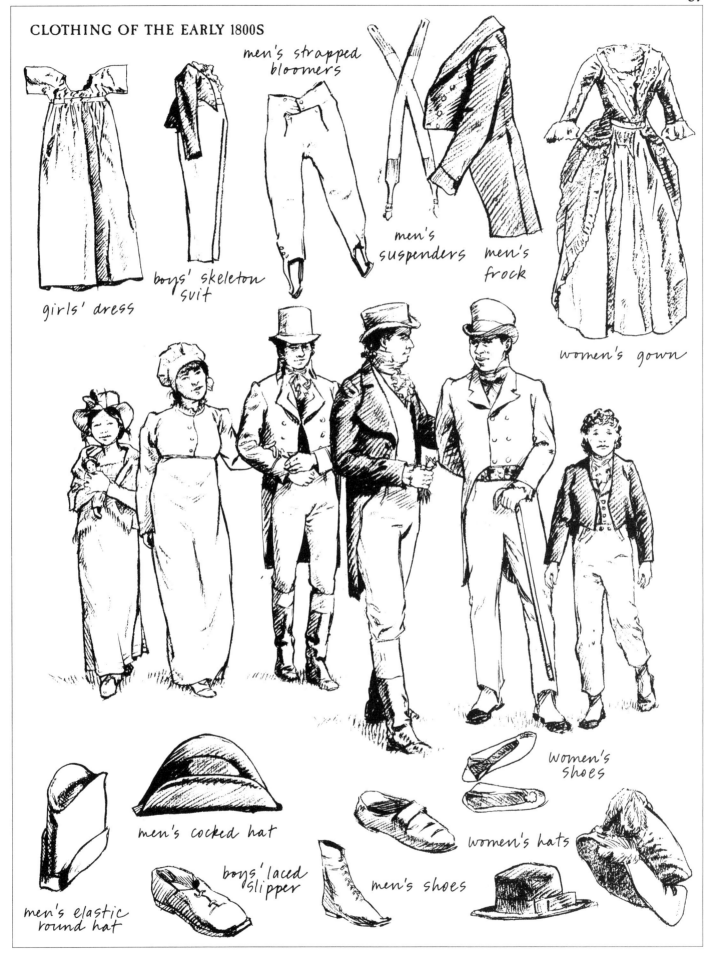

girls' dress

boys' skeleton suit

men's strapped bloomers

men's suspenders

men's frock

women's gown

men's cocked hat

women's shoes

men's elastic round hat

boys' laced slipper

men's shoes

women's hats

HOW TO SUCCEED IN CONGRESS

John Caldwell Calhoun's father was a plantation owner and state legislator in South Carolina. John was just twelve when his father died. The family's cotton plantations became the boy's to manage. One day a neighbor spotted young John working in the field with a book tied to his plow. It wasn't long after this that his two older brothers came home for a visit. They thought he should become a lawyer.

John said he would, if they would pay for the best education America could give him. He would need seven years for academy, college, and law school. His brothers consented.

In 1802 John entered Yale College, one of the finest schools in New England. He concentrated on reasoning, logic, and debate. One day the president of Yale, Dr. Timothy Dwight, visited John's philosophy class, and soon he and John were debating politics. Neither could change the other's mind. Dr. Dwight remarked later that it would not surprise him if John Calhoun were one day the president of the United States.

John graduated near the top of his class at Yale and began law school. When he finished in 1807, he opened his office in a red log cabin in Abbeville, South Carolina. The same year, he got the break that determined how he would make a living.

That spring, a British warship shelled an American vessel off the Virginia coast. A group of townspeople asked Calhoun to write to Congress about the attack. It did not take the young lawyer long to discover that he loved politics. A few months later, John Calhoun was their favorite candidate for a seat in the South Carolina legislature. With this win, he began planning his next move. His eye was on the President's House.

Three summers later, he asked his distant cousin, Floride Colhoun, to marry him. (She spelled her last name differently.) He also visited the neighborhoods of his political district, asking his friends to vote for him for Congress. In September 1810 he won the election by a large majority. As he waited impatiently for his wedding day, Senator John Calhoun had everything a young statesman could want.

Young John working in the field, with a book tied to his plow.

A Wedding at Bonneau's Plantation

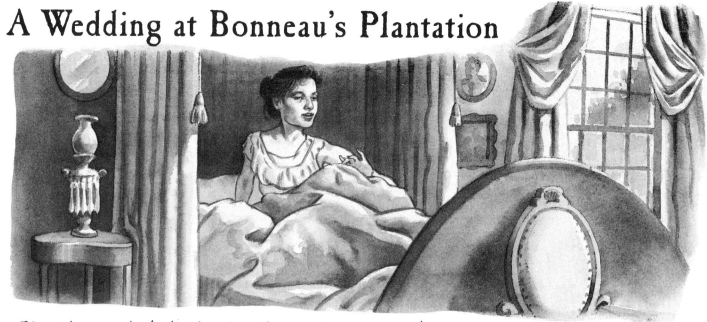

Floride pushed back the blue satin comforter.

Dawn rose over the fields and gardens of Bonneau's plantation. A green lawn circled the stately Colhoun mansion, with its wide front porch and tall white columns. For the wealthy Colhoun family, the day usually began slowly. But on this January morning in 1811, everyone was up. The two black house servants, Josephine and Ruth, wearing their starched uniforms and white aprons, hurried through the house, opening the shutters that hid the tall windows. Sunlight streaked across thick carpets, fine furniture, and walls of portraits and landscape paintings in their carved frames.

In her bedroom, on the second floor, Floride (Flor-EED) Colhoun pushed back the blue satin comforter. She ran her hands over her face, trying to wake up. All night long she had tossed and tangled the blankets, never really sleeping. She would not have her daily nap this afternoon, either. Instead, there would be a hundred guests and more, some of whom were already here. Most would remain long into the night, dancing and celebrating. This was Floride's wedding day.

The slender nineteen-year-old girl threw on her morning robe and went downstairs. She had no appetite for breakfast. The wide hallway was already decorated for her wedding with pale gray branches of wild olive. She found her mother in the large reception room where the ceremony would be held. Mrs. Colhoun was supervising Lucas and Johnny. Their dark arms held long boughs of magnolias whose large pale buds had begun to unfold. They arranged the branches in tall vases beside the hearth and windows. Fresh holly and early-blooming jasmine covered the mantel and lined the mirrors. A sweet scent filled the room.

Mrs. Colhoun embraced her daughter, brushing back Floride's dark, tangled hair. "Darling, you look tired. Did you sleep at all? Are you overexcited?"

Floride was about to answer when she heard the deep, familiar voice of John Calhoun coming from the back hallway. It was bad luck for the groom to see his bride until just before the ceremony. Floride didn't think of herself as superstitious, but she wanted this day to be perfect. She turned from her mother without answering and rushed upstairs to her bedroom.

Lying across the four-poster bed were her silk stockings, long lace veil, and wedding gown. Lifting up the white dress, she ran her finger over the smooth satin, the tiny pearl trim, and the imported lace. The high bodice and scooped neckline were very stylish. Even the color—white—was the latest fashion. Among her friends, she would be the first to be married in white. She wanted it that way. She liked being ahead of style and capturing attention when she attended dances in Charleston. She couldn't wait to see the guests' eyes today when she appeared in her gown. Most of all, she wanted to please Mr. Calhoun.

The house was cool, and Floride shivered. She could have chosen a summer wedding, but she thought January was the best month to be married in. She remembered the childhood verse from her Scottish and Irish heritage:

Marry when the year is new,
Always loving, always true.

She knew Mr. Calhoun would be a good husband. John Calhoun was her distant cousin. Floride was just a child when he first came to visit her family. After her father died, he often spent his vacations with them, helping Mrs. Colhoun and playing with Floride's brothers. Her mother was very fond of him. She believed the young man would be a great leader some day.

Floride didn't care much for politics, but she was eager to be married and settled in her own house. They would have fine dinners and wonderful parties. She could sew, make soap and candles, and she could already manage a household of slaves. As she thought about the new life that awaited her, she worried only about controlling her fiery temper. But John Calhoun loved her and promised he would be patient. She hoped she would make a good wife.

From her bedroom window, Floride watched her cousins arrive. Carriages and buggies stopped in the wide drive. Ladies in velvet capes and flower-print dresses swept up the steps, escorted by husbands in long waistcoats and ruffled shirts. The guests gathered in the reception room.

Floride watched her cousins arrive.

Their new life together had begun.

As Floride was dressing, her mother appeared in her room, to put the final touches on her hair and to arrange her veil. Mrs. Colhoun pinned the lace in place and gave her only daughter a long hug. When the young bride was finally ready, they went down the stairs together, and into the back parlor.

Mrs. Colhoun disappeared to look for the groom so he and Floride could spend a few minutes alone together before the ceremony. The bride had a small gift for her new husband. It was her portrait, painted in miniature and set in a tiny frame.

In the reception room, the guests listened as a lovely young girl played the harp. Her fingers plucked the strings gently, creating a dreamy, beautiful melody. John Caldwell Calhoun and one of his older brothers entered the room and stood beside the fireplace. Like Floride, Calhoun was slender and dark-eyed. He was twenty-nine, ten years older than Floride. He stood six feet two inches tall, with a mass of thick black hair, piercing eyes, high cheekbones, and a strong jaw. The senator was a stranger to many of the guests. Someone whispered that last September he had been elected to Congress by a landslide.

Everyone turned as the bride entered the room. She walked beside her uncle, their arms linked. The long satin train of her gown swept silently across the floor. The lace veil fell over Floride's face to her shoulders, hiding her eyes. A wreath of white orange blossoms crowned her long hair, and she carried a single white rose.

The bride walked to the fireplace, where John Calhoun stood waiting. Floride looked up at him. Through her veil, John saw a shy smile on her lips. The music ended. The room fell silent. The handsome couple faced the minister and spoke the vows that made them husband and wife. Their new life together had begun.

A DECISION AT FORT HILL

In 1811 John Calhoun went to Washington to serve in Congress. He was devoted to the South, but in politics he put the good of the whole nation first. Those who predicted he would be successful were right. President James Monroe appointed him secretary of war in 1817. Calhoun kept this position until 1824, when Monroe's second term as president ended.

Five men ran for president in 1824, and John Calhoun was one of them. But when he counted the votes he expected to receive, he didn't have enough to win. He was forty-two years old, still young for a president. He thought he could wait. He dropped out of the presidential race, ran for vice president, and was easily elected.

For the next eight years, Calhoun served with President John Quincy Adams. The Calhouns lived in Georgetown, near Washington. Their home, owned by Floride's mother, was a stately mansion, now called Dumbarton Oaks. It had thirty acres of gardens, woods, grapevines, and fruit trees.

Calhoun was happy, but he longed to raise his children in South Carolina, where he had grown up. In 1826 his wish came true. He moved his family to Clemson, South Carolina. Their new home was a cotton plantation Floride's father had owned. Calhoun renamed the property Fort Hill, to remember a post that had been built

He sat rocking on the porch.

there during the Revolutionary War. The two-story mansion with tall white columns stood at the end of a shady driveway, overlooking the Seneca River.

At Fort Hill, Calhoun improved the way he planted corn, invented a better plow, and experimented with weed control in his fields. He helped his children plant little gardens of their own. He enjoyed watching hummingbirds flit through the flowers and picking ripe peaches and pears from his trees.

As he sat rocking on the porch, he thought about America's problems—and his own. Calhoun's biggest problem wasn't the work he had to do. He and Floride owned thirty slaves or more, and from what we know, they seem to have been treated well. The trouble at Fort Hill was money. Floride bought beautiful clothes, and the Calhouns often had extra guests at dinner. They also had seven children to feed, clothe, and educate.

The biggest drain on his money, Calhoun believed, was an import tax, called a tariff, that people in the northern states—and even Calhoun, when he was younger—had voted for. Tariffs protected industries in the North from competing with certain products that could be made more cheaply in England and France. They helped American industries by adding a few cents to the price of some imported goods, making them cost the same as similar things made in the United States.

But like other Southerners, Calhoun began to see how the tariff raised prices on many things he bought. After many years of voting for tariffs, now Calhoun thought they should be stopped.

Calhoun was against the right of states in one part of America to pass laws—like tariff laws—that were good for them if those laws were bad for people in another part of the country. This *regionalism*, where one section of the country cared only about its own welfare, instead of what was best for the entire nation, made Calhoun angry.

In 1827 Congress was stopped by a tie vote. Should the members pass a new tariff on wool? Vice President Calhoun must cast the deciding vote. In a decision that upset many New Englanders, he voted against the tariff. His vote made him unpopular in the North, and he lost the chance to become president in 1828. Andrew Jackson won the election, and again Calhoun had to settle for being the vice president.

The People's Choice

No one wanted to miss this historic day, March 4, 1829. Today Americans would witness the inauguration of the seventh president of the United States. Andrew Jackson was his name. He was an ordinary American. He was the people's choice.

The people had watched six presidents come and go—all easterners. With each succeeding president, government corruption increased. No one seemed able to stop it. The people were fed up.

Government officials stole money; $500,000 was taken from the U.S. Treasury—and that was just one government department. Officials gave businessmen opportunities to profit while ignoring the common citizens' needs. Even John Adams, the outgoing president, was accused of using the people's money to purchase a pool table.

No more! For the first time a man from the West was elected president. Andrew Jackson wasn't a gentleman from Virginia or Massachusetts. He was no businessman. He was a frontiersman from Tennessee and a military hero. He was a common citizen who was going to get government to listen to the people.

Never had such a fuss been made over the inauguration of an American president. People from all over the world flocked to the capital. Hotel rooms were crammed with visitors. Six people shared a bed. People were happy to sleep on pool tables, floors, or in doorways.

"Jackson men" invaded the city. They were frontiersmen with buckskin on their backs, mud on their boots, and whiskey on their breath.

As the noontime inauguration neared, Andrew Jackson left the Gadsby Hotel. Cannon fire greeted his appearance. A loud cheer rang out from the sea of people waiting for him.

Jackson stood on the steps of his hotel, his tall, slender frame there for all to see. Dressed in a plain black suit, he stared out at the crowd with his steel-blue eyes. His stand-on-end white hair was half combed and most likely greased with bear's oil, as was the habit of many men at that time.

Jackson joined the crowds in the people-packed street. He walked to the Capitol surrounded by carts, wagons, and throngs of well-

"Jackson men" invaded the city.

wishers and job seekers hoping to speak to him about employment in the government.

Noontime. The inauguration began. John Calhoun, Jackson's vice president, was sworn in first in the Senate chambers. Now it was Jackson's turn. A procession marched from the chambers to the east portico, or porch, where 20,000 people awaited Jackson's appearance.

Suddenly the doors swung open. Marshals paraded out. Justices of the Supreme Court came out next. Nearby, members of the marine band took their places. Then Jackson came into view! A chorus of yells erupted from the crowd. Margaret Bayard, the wife of a Maryland senator, later wrote, "All hats were off at once, and the dark tint which usually pervades a mixed map of men was turned . . . into the bright hue of ten thousand upturned and exultant human faces, radiant with sudden joy."

Jackson gave his acceptance speech, but very few people beyond the first rows heard him. His speech lasted ten minutes, one of the shortest

The Two-Party System

By the time James Madison became the president in 1809, the two-party political system, inspired by Jefferson and Hamilton, had been reduced to one political party, the Democratic-Republican party.

Many people felt the one-party system had caused government to become corrupt. Without a second party, there was no opposition to challenge dishonest politicians.

With the hope of Jackson becoming the president, a new party was created, and the two-party system was renewed. The new party was called the Democratic Party. The established party changed its name to the National Republicans.

ever. The crowd showered him with applause. In turn, Jackson offered his thanks.

The oath of office was given by the chief justice. When it was over, Jackson would officially be the president of the United States. The people listened, trying to control their enthusiasm. When the last word was spoken, they could restrain themselves no longer.

The crowd rushed forward and surrounded their president. Marshals ushered President Jackson inside the Capitol to protect him from the people. It was a wasted effort. The president had to travel back up Pennsylvania Avenue to the White House, his new home, for a public reception.

President Jackson mounted a white horse and rode to the White House followed by "country men, farmers, gentlemen, mounted and dismounted, boys, women and children, black and white."

When he arrived at his new residence, he found a riot going on. People were crammed

into the house. Men grabbed barrels of punch from waiters' hands. Glasses and chinaware smashed to the ground. Spilled whiskey scented the air. Gentlemen and ladies were trapped in the people's merriment.

Children romped about. Men gave each other bloody noses. Women passed out. Frontiersmen stood in "boots heavy with mud" on "damask satin-covered chairs," trying to see President Jackson over the crazed crowd.

People swarmed around the president, almost smothering him to death with affection. Friends formed a protective circle around Jackson and escorted him from the party.

His leaving didn't stop the celebration. This party was for the people. The ordinary citizens finally felt they had elected a president who was just like them.

When it was over, it took days to clear away the mess and make necessary repairs. Never before or since has a president been welcomed with such riotous affection.

When he arrived, he found a riot going on.

"OLD HICKORY"

Before Andrew Jackson became president, he was a general in the United States Army. Most soldiers called him by his nickname, "Old Hickory."

He was given this unusual nickname during the War of 1812. During the bitter winter of 1813, Jackson received orders to march his men to New Orleans to help General Wilkinson. When he arrived, the general ordered Jackson and his men to camp some distance from the headquarters in New Orleans.

Jackson waited weeks for his orders; finally, they came. But not from General Wilkinson. The new secretary of war, John Armstrong, ordered Jackson to dismiss his troops. They were no longer needed. No further explanation was given, just, "Accept for yourself and the Corps the thanks of the President and the United States."

The command was baffling, but it couldn't be disobeyed. Jackson was furious. This was unbelievable! He had brought his men 800 miles only to be dismissed without pay or food.

General Jackson rallied his men to march back home. Jackson used $1,000 of his own money to buy eleven wagons to carry the sick. As soldiers slashed their way through the wilderness, Jackson moved up and down the columns of soldiers on foot, helping the sick and passing out food.

His men were impressed by Jackson's toughness. One soldier called him "tough as hickory." The comparison was a fitting one. From that time on, Andrew Jackson was known as "Old Hickory."

A MAN OF SPIRIT

Americans truly believed President Andrew Jackson was a common person just like them. When he became president, he wasn't poor like most Americans, though. He was a wealthy Tennessee planter, a slave owner, and a lawyer. That didn't matter. What most Americans cared about was Jackson's spirited nature. They weren't interested in the fact that Jackson studied law. What appealed to Americans were the tales of young Andrew Jackson's law training.

Jackson loved horses and parties. When he was training to be a lawyer, in Salisbury, North Carolina, he spent a lot of time at the Salisbury dance school and the local tavern.

Some people disapproved of Jackson's behavior—especially for a future president. But many adventurous Americans respected him. America was a country of people on the move, making new homes in new territories. Life was a rough adventure. Most people had no problem relating to Jackson's rambunctious behavior, even when his actions almost started a war between the United States and Spain.

In 1818 Florida was part of the nation of Spain. Runaway slaves commonly fled to Florida because they knew American troops wouldn't enter Spanish territory. Congress feared such an action would cause Spain to declare war on the United States. Seminole Indians living in Florida also took advantage of this fact. They frequently attacked southern farms without fear of retaliation by the United States.

Jackson didn't care about causing a war. He had had enough of runaway slaves and Indian attacks. He commanded his troops to cross into Florida, where they captured Spanish forts, including one fort hiding two Indian chiefs. The chiefs were hanged. By the time Jackson and his men were finished, they had brought all of eastern Florida under the control of the United States.

Americans cheered Jackson. But some members of Congress were furious. Jackson might have started a war. Instead, Jackson's attack made the Spanish government realize it could no longer defend Florida. In 1819 Spain sold Florida to the United States.

Corruption Must Go

President Jackson fought government corruption. He fired dishonest officials and ordered the heads of every government department to create an efficient, more honorable government.

Jackson also proposed legislation to prevent officials from becoming corrupt. He believed that the longer officials stayed in office, the more they cared about themselves and the less they cared about the people they were supposed to serve. Jackson suggested that officials shouldn't serve more than four years in the government.

Today, many people are still disturbed by the corruption of some government officials. Several states have recently passed laws limiting how long government officials can serve in hopes of creating a more responsible government. We are still trying to solve some of the same problems faced by Andrew Jackson.

The Trail Where They Wept

Gold on Indian Land

The Cherokee Nation and the United States signed the Hopewell Treaty in 1785. This treaty guaranteed that Cherokee land in Georgia, Alabama, North Carolina, and Tennessee wouldn't be invaded by whites.

In July 1829, gold was discovered thirty miles from New Echota, the capital of the Cherokee Nation. Americans invaded the Cherokee Nation searching for gold. The Georgia legislature took away the Cherokee's legal rights to the gold and to protest the legislature's action.

Georgian lawmakers shouldn't have denied the Cherokee their legal rights. The Cherokee Nation was a sovereign nation. The United States government had said so.

Cherokee lawyers took their complaints to the Supreme Court and to President Jackson. But neither the president or the court would interfere with the Georgia legislature.

In July 1830, the U.S. Congress passed the Indian Removal Act. This act ordered the Cherokee to leave their land for a new home in the Oklahoma Territory.

Cherokee leaders didn't want to leave. On December 28, 1837, two U.S. officials issued a statement giving the Cherokee less than five months to leave their homeland for the Oklahoma Territory.

Indians often called this bitter journey to their new home "The Trail Where They Wept."

The Cherokee girl looked at the Mississippi River. She clutched her doll. She didn't want to cross the river. Water was the entrance to the underworld. Traveling on the river could anger the spirits. But the girl had no choice. She must cross the river and trust the shaman, a spiritual leader, to calm the spirits.

There were a thousand people in her group. It would take days for the ferry to transport everyone to the other side. Holding back her tears, the girl helped her mother set up camp.

She had lived in a camp before. For two months she waited in one with her family and 2,000 other people. Thousands of other Cherokee people stayed in similar camps along the Georgia and Tennessee border. They all waited in the summer heat to travel to their new home. The Cherokee Nation had surrendered their old homeland. White people wanted the territory.

A treaty was signed by Indian and American leaders. The Cherokee gave up the land in which their ancestors were buried. In return the U.S. government paid for removal of those living on this land. They also gave the people money and promises of further assistance.

The treaty meant nothing to the Cherokee girl. She missed her home, the smell of sassafras root, and the joy of the corn harvest. She missed the taste of sweet corn soup made from young kernels. She missed the sound of songs being sung giving thanks for the bountiful crop.

She hated the camp. It was a dangerous home. Garbage and human waste brought sickness to her people. She was surrounded by death and the sounds of women weeping and the shaman's mournful chanting.

One day her father developed a fever. A white doctor offered him medicine. He refused it. Her father preferred to die. Five days later he was dead. Her father's attitude was common. Many Indians hated the whites. They would rather die than accept the whites' help.

The girl thought of her father as she crossed the river the next day. The spirits of the dead moved west, just as she was doing. She held her doll and prayed her father wasn't angry if he was watching.

Many days later, when everyone had crossed the river, the Cherokee continued on their journey. They followed the westward trail. The sky was cloudless. There was no relief from the sun's heat. The earth was dry and brittle. Wagons, people, and animals kicked up dust as they moved. The air was thick with it. The girl coughed as she walked, carrying her bundle. Hundreds of people coughed. Babies cried. Elders collapsed.

Still they went forward, from one day to the next, leaving behind their buried dead and a land whose grasses had been devoured by the wagon animals.

Every evening, as the sun set, the wagons stopped, and the dust settled. It was time to rest, pray, and eat. The girl ate the same meal of salted pork and bread. She wiped her family's utensils and bowls with a dirty rag. She took her doll and lay down on the ground, covering herself with a threadbare blanket.

Weeks later, thunder boomed in the sky and rain fell. Fall had come. In an instant the dry earth turned to mud beneath the people's feet and the wagons' wheels. Wheels broke as they moved over uneven, sloppy land. The girl was soaked and caked in mud. She would stay wet until the sun came out again.

Eventually fall gave way to winter. The wind blew cold from the north. The wet ground stored the cold. Creeks surrendered to it and froze over.

The girl coughed constantly. At night, her body ached from sleeping on the frozen ground. After ninety days of traveling, she was exhausted.

The girl grew weaker with each day of winter. There was nothing her mother could do for her, just as there was nothing she could do to stop this journey.

One evening, under a cold starry night, the girl curled up with her doll and died. Her mother wept, as so many mothers had already.

More than 16,000 Cherokee men, women, and children traveled 1,000 miles in winter's bitter cold to their new home. More than 4,000 Cherokee people died in camps and on the "Trail Where They Wept."

One evening the girl curled up with her doll and died.

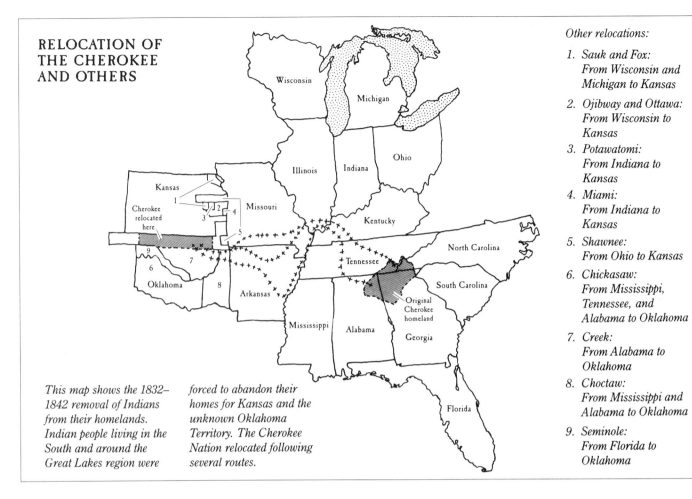

RELOCATION OF
THE CHEROKEE
AND OTHERS

Wisconsin
Michigan
Illinois
Indiana
Ohio
Kansas
Missouri
Kentucky
North Carolina
Cherokee relocated here
Tennessee
South Carolina
Oklahoma
Arkansas
Original Cherokee homeland
Mississippi
Alabama
Georgia
Florida

This map shows the 1832–1842 removal of Indians from their homelands. Indian people living in the South and around the Great Lakes region were forced to abandon their homes for Kansas and the unknown Oklahoma Territory. The Cherokee Nation relocated following several routes.

Other relocations:

1. *Sauk and Fox: From Wisconsin and Michigan to Kansas*
2. *Ojibway and Ottawa: From Wisconsin to Kansas*
3. *Potawatomi: From Indiana to Kansas*
4. *Miami: From Indiana to Kansas*
5. *Shawnee: From Ohio to Kansas*
6. *Chickasaw: From Mississippi, Tennessee, and Alabama to Oklahoma*
7. *Creek: From Alabama to Oklahoma*
8. *Choctaw: From Mississippi and Alabama to Oklahoma*
9. *Seminole: From Florida to Oklahoma*

WE DID WHAT YOU ASKED

Time and time again, American leaders wanted the Indian people to live as Americans did. Some Cherokee people did just that. Many of them lived in log cabins or fine wooden homes. They wore American-style clothing and prayed in churches. Some of the Cherokee owned black slaves, just as their southern white neighbors did.

John Ridge, a leader in the Cherokee Nation, said, "You asked us to throw off the hunter and warrior state: We did so. You asked us to form a republican government: We did so, adopting your own as a model. You asked us to cultivate the earth, and learn the mechanics arts: We did so. You asked us to learn to read: We did so. You asked us to cast away our idols, and worship your God: We did so."

The Cherokee people's effort to act like Americans was not enough. The United States government wanted the Cherokee homeland, and they would have it. Most Americans, President Jackson among them, strongly believed that no one, including the Cherokee people, had the right to stop America from getting what it wanted.

Not everyone felt this way. There were people who were against the Indian Removal Act. Newspapers, authors, missionaries, and ordinary citizens all expressed their anger and disgust.

An English geologist, while staying near an Indian camp in Georgia, said, "A whole Indian nation . . . adopts the Christian religion, uses books printed in their own language . . . relies on agriculture for their support, and produces men of great ability to rule over them. . . . Are not these the great principles of civilization? [The Cherokee] are driven from their . . . state then, not because they cannot be civilized, but because . . . beings who are too strong for them, want their possessions!"

American general John Ellis Wool pitied the Indians. He felt they should be removed for their own safety. He said, "If I could . . . I would remove every Indian tomorrow, beyond the reach of the white men, who like vultures are watching, ready to pounce upon their prey, and strip them of everything they have."

Finally, many Americans, living in eastern cities, had no idea what all the fuss was about. They had never heard of the Cherokee Nation, nor had they ever met or traded with Indians.

The Land of White Gold

The Georgia sun beamed down across Jo's back. Gnats swarmed around his face. Sometimes they got so close he breathed them into his mouth. Sweat ran down his forehead. Lice crawled through his matted black hair. He did not stop plowing to wipe his forehead or to scratch his scalp. He kept on, breaking up the dry, red earth. Ahead of him, the mule slowly dragged the plow. Jo held the handles firmly, digging the row as straight as he could. Every time his bare feet hit a sharp rock or a stubble from last year's cotton crop, pain shot into his skin.

It was hard breaking the soil to plant cotton. Jo had never plowed before. But he liked working alone, in charge of something big. Across the field he saw clouds of dust from other plows. But he felt alone under the bright blue sky. Overhead, huge piles of clouds floated silently along. The breeze refreshed him. Jo noticed puffs of gray among the white. Rain might fall before dark.

The weather was always changing, but you could plan on it growing warmer every week. Where the field was plowed, other slaves sowed the seeds. It was backbreaking work. All day long, they bent over, pushing each seed one inch into the soil, covering it, and moving on. Watering would come next, and eventually chopping, during the worst of summer's heat. Every slave the master owned would be needed to hoe, or "chop," the young cotton plants, thinning and weeding them. Finally, when the fields looked like pillows of soft bedding, picking began. "White gold," men called this crop. It was the wealth of the South. But Jo knew it would never make him rich.

The master's leather bullwhip snapped in the air.

A little whirlwind swirled over the field, filling the boy's eyes and mouth with dust. He blinked. His eyelids scraped against his eyes like sandpaper. His mouth was too dry to spit. The fine grit coated his teeth. When he moved his jaw, dirt crunched between his teeth. Inside his head, it sounded as if he were chewing rocks.

At the edge of the field, Jo recognized the form of his master on horseback. The man's voice boomed angrily. His leather bullwhip snapped in the air. Jo flinched, trying to ignore the helpless wails of the slaves who felt the master's anger across their backs, splitting skin into raw grooves of flesh. Today Jo might be lucky and escape a whipping himself, for the twelve-year-old was doing a man's work, toiling as hard as he could. But often, he knew, even the best effort was rewarded with cruelty.

All afternoon, Jo guided the plow along the endless rows. The world was silent, except for the muffled clomp of the mule's hooves and the scratch of soil and stones sliding off the blades of the plow. He did not know how many rows he had plowed; he couldn't count. But as far as he could see, the land stretched away in rough ribbons of broken earth.

He was allowed to stop once for a ten-minute rest and a drink of water. When the plantation bell rang, he dropped the plow and trudged across the field. Everyone had stopped working. When it was his turn to drink, Jo dipped the long-handled ladle into the water bucket and took a big gulp. He lay down in a patch of weeds and closed his eyes. With his stomach growling in hunger and his muscles aching, he fell asleep.

The Cotton Gin

If it hadn't been for a machine invented in 1793, slavery might have been abolished many years earlier than it finally was. In the 1800s cotton became more important in the South than rice or tobacco, especially in Georgia and South Carolina. It was shipped to textile mills in northern states such as Massachusetts and across the Atlantic to the factories in England.

Cleaning the cotton after it was picked was a slow job. It took a whole day for a slave to pick all the seeds out of one pound of cotton.

That changed when Eli Whitney introduced his new hand-turned machine, or engine, nicknamed the cotton "gin." The cotton gin made it possible for one slave to clean 50 pounds of cotton in a day. When it was improved again to run by steam power, it could clean 1,000 pounds in the same amount of time. Suddenly cotton was even more profitable. Everyone was planting it, and, ironically, more slaves were needed to pick it.

"Git up, you worthless dog!" the master hissed. Jo opened his eyes, gasping for air and coughing water from his lungs. The master who stood over him had emptied a pail of water in his face. The boy scrambled up. He saw the bucket coming as the master swung it toward him, but it was too late. It hit him in the head like a clap of thunder. Jo doubled over in pain. As he slumped to the ground, he did not feel the blood flowing down the side of his head.

When the master had gone, Jeb ran to Jo's side. He pulled off his shirt and gently wrapped it around his friend's head, trying not to disturb him. He couldn't stay with Jo—if the master saw him doing this, Jeb knew he would feel the whip harder than ever. He had to get back to the field before he was missed. But he would return when the quitting bell rang, to help carry Jo home.

At night, the two boys often met outside in the darkness. After a supper of grits and bacon, they hid in the shadows of a stand of pine trees. No one saw them. They talked in low voices, about going fishing on Sundays, or hunting with Jo's uncle, or about how much they hated the master.

That night Jo appeared. His head was still wrapped in the bloody cloth. He told Jeb a secret. Soon he was going to run away. He was figuring out which way to go without being caught. One way or another, he told Jeb, he would escape to the North, where he would be free.

At first, Jeb thought Jo was crazy. Running away was dangerous and stupid. He agreed with Jo that life here was hard. But Jeb argued that they were treated better here than many of their people elsewhere. It was risky to try to escape. Jo and Jeb both knew that when runaway slaves were caught, they were severely punished.

The boys crept back through the dark to their cabins. As Jeb lay on the dirt floor trying to fall asleep, he thought about Jo's plan. After what had happened today, he didn't think running away was so crazy anymore. But he wondered how badly Jo had been hurt by the bucket. If Jo *could* go—when he was okay and if he still wanted to— Jeb decided he would go, too. He finally fell asleep, thinking tomorrow might be the last day he would ever drop cotton seeds into the ground.

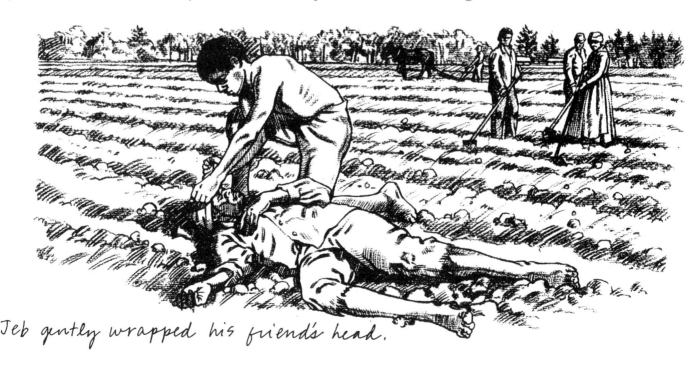

Jeb gently wrapped his friend's head.

A MASTER AND A FRIEND

Charles Minor was born in Virginia in 1805. When he was a child of three, an elderly friend of the family gave him a young black boy. Ralph was almost the same age as Charles, and the two boys played together like brothers. Charles was taught to share his toys with Ralph and use good manners with him as he would with anyone else. As Charles grew up, his family began to question their right to "own" other people. One by one, they helped their slaves find ways to make a living and gave them their freedom. Granting a slave his or her freedom was called "manumission." In 1832 Ralph was manumitted by this letter, written by Charles Minor.

Dear Ralph,

I am no longer your master, but I am still your friend, and as perhaps we shall never meet again, I have determined to give you this assurance of my esteem.

You have ever maintained a character for honesty and gentlemanly deportment [behavior], and I trust that now you are free you will never give me cause to blush for having emancipated one who was unworthy of it.

You were my playmate and nurse and the good will which you won of me in my boyish days is still warmly cherished, and if I ever hear of your being otherwise than a Virginia gentleman, I shall be grievously disappointed.

I have once said it, and here repeat it: I pronounce you free in the name of Almighty God.

I strongly advise you to go to Liberia and if you will do so I will add fifty dollars to your earnings.

If you go to Tennessee you will very probably be taken up and sold to the highest bidder. . . . At Liberia you may become one of the first gentlemen of the country. . . . You must write to me as often as you can.

No more your master but always your friend,

Charles L. C. Minor, U.S. Army

Charles warned Ralph to show this letter only in small groups where he had witnesses. This would prevent someone from taking away the letter that proved he was free.

We don't know where Ralph decided to go. He had learned a trade. He could earn money perhaps by doing carpentry or blacksmith work. Charles hoped he would go to Liberia, a country in Africa. Some white Southerners had started a colony of former slaves there. They believed that blacks in America would never be treated equally, but in the land of their ancestors they could live as they wanted to. Charles's brother Lancelot was a minister who spent several years in the colony, helping to get it organized.

The colony did not succeed. For one thing, it was expensive to send the ships and supplies that were needed to build homes and stores. Not enough people donated to the cause. But a bigger problem was that most blacks who had grown up in America were not excited about going to a strange land. They would have to give up everything and leave almost everyone they knew to start over in a foreign country. They didn't agree with white people who thought it would be like going "home." America was home.

Family Patches

Charles Ball, a free black man, wrote a book in 1836 about slavery in America. He said that everywhere he went, the slaves he met were allowed to plant their own gardens, which were called "patches," in a corner of the master's property where the soil wasn't useful for much else. Usually this meant in the woods, where shade and undergrowth kept plants from growing to their maximum. Even so, the blacks planted corn, potatoes, pumpkins, melons, and other crops. The only day they could take care of their own patches was Sunday, when they weren't working for their owners.

THE SLAVE TRADE IN AMERICA

The first Africans were kidnapped from their homeland and brought to the colonies in 1619. In 1808 Congress passed a law that stopped Americans from bringing more slaves to the United States. But by the Civil War, when slavery was completely abolished in America, there were more than 4 million slaves in the United States. Most were the children or grandchildren of slaves captured in Africa.

Africans who were captured against their will and sold into slavery faced terrible hardships. Thousands died during their voyage to America. They were chained together below the decks of the ships that carried them. They had no room to sit or lie down, and no toilets or a place to wash. There was little fresh air or water, and the food was unfit for animals. Those who survived the ocean crossing were auctioned off at the docks when they arrived in America. Families were torn apart, their names were changed, and slaves who resisted these cruelties were whipped and sometimes left for dead.

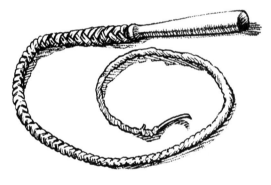

MISSOURI IN THE MIDDLE

Since colonial days, people had argued about slavery without finding a solution. In general, most Americans in the northern states wanted slavery ended, or abolished. People in the southern states wanted it continued, since the farms and plantations in the South depended on slavery for their survival.

By 1819, twenty-two states made up the United States of America. They happened to be divided equally between "slave" and "free." When Congress voted on issues, this balance meant that neither section of the country held too much power. But in 1819 the Missouri Territory wanted to become a slave state—a state where slavery was permitted. People knew there would be problems when the balance was lost.

After months of debate, Congress found a solution called the Missouri Compromise. It allowed slaves in the new state of Missouri, but to keep the balance, another new state, Maine, was created. It entered the Union as a "free" state.

Congress also ruled that slavery would be illegal in all territory north of the latitude 36°30′. One reason southern states accepted the compromise was that explorers who had seen this land said it was mainly desert. Southerners didn't think slaves would be needed to work in such poor fields.

When the agreement was reached, Missouri entered the union in 1820 as the twenty-fourth state. The immediate problem was settled, but the issue of keeping slaves in America was far from resolved.

"THE BAYONET SHALL PIERCE ME THROUGH"

Maria W. Stewart was a free black woman. Her husband was killed during the War of 1812, and dishonorable lawyers cheated her out of his government pension. Mrs. Stewart was well educated and held strong views about the injustices in America. In 1833 she spoke to an audience in Boston. She may very likely be the first woman to speak in public in the United States. Her talk was published in a newspaper and in a book of her writings. Most people did not want to hear what she had to say. They made her so uncomfortable, she stopped speaking in public. But her words carried the truth. This is the end of one of her speeches, in which she talks about sending blacks back to Liberia:

"The unfriendly whites first drove the native American from his much loved home. Then they stole our fathers from their peaceful and quiet dwellings, and brought them hither [here] and made bond men and bond women out of them and their little ones; they have obliged our brethren [brothers] to labor, [they] keep them in utter ignorance . . . and now that we have enriched their soil, and filled their coffers [pockets and banks] they say that we are not capable of becoming like white men, and that we can never rise to respectability in this country. They would drive us to a strange land. But before I go, the bayonet shall pierce me through. African rights and liberty is a subject that ought to fire the breast of every free man of color in these United States, and excite in his bosom a lively, deep, decided and heart-felt interest."

A Baby on Her Back

Charles Ball remembered how slave women worked in the fields and cared for their babies at the same time. He wrote that mothers took their babies with them every morning. They laid the infants down at the end of the cotton row they were planting or weeding. When the slaves were permitted to stop for a drink of water, the mothers went straight to their babies and nursed them. Their friends brought them water in empty gourd shells.

One mother figured out a way to keep her baby with her all day. She tied a large piece of fabric loosely around her body and tucked the baby inside it. With the baby safe on her back, she could hoe all day but still do what mattered most to her—take care of her child.

Hannie's First Week

Standing for thirteen hours a day hurt Hannie's feet.

Hannie placed the baby mouse in her hat, covered it with her nightgown, and slid it under her bed. She clattered down the boardinghouse stairs and raced to the mill. As she reached the steps, the bell stopped ringing.

Hannie pulled at the door. It was locked. She pounded until her fists hurt, but no one came. She sat down and wiped her sweaty face on her apron. Hannie's name would go on the slate inside the building again. Hannie already knew about the slate. It held the names of girls who came to work late, worked too slowly, or made careless mistakes. Hannie's name had been written on the slate once already. Now everyone would see it there again. And all because she had saved a tiny mouse. It wasn't fair.

Hannie was new at the textile factory. Monday had been her first day. An older girl from the boardinghouse had shown her the work. Hannie was ten. Her first job had been filling bobbins. Then she'd learned how to change the empty spools. Soon she would learn to operate the weaver. Filling bobbins and changing empty spools was easy, but standing for thirteen hours a day hurt her feet. Huge spinning mules on the lower floors banged all day, and the weavers pounded like thunder. Her head throbbed. That first night, she could barely finish her supper. She had fallen asleep before the curfew bell.

The second day she had filled bobbins again. By noon, her feet hurt badly. She decided to skip lunch and go wading instead, to soothe her swollen toes. She thought she would have time, but then the warning bell rang and she raced back to the mill.

Hannie had discovered the marsh the Sunday before, with Katie, another new girl. After church they explored it together. Hannie loved the marsh. It was alive with red-winged blackbirds, turtles, and bugs that spun tiny circles on the water.

When Hannie had gone back to the marsh by herself on Tuesday, she'd discovered a nest of baby ducklings. She forgot her hunger as she watched them sleeping. She spotted the mother mallard nearby, bobbing under the water for food. Hannie crouched

Mill Girls

Sometimes an entire family went to work at one of the many mills in New England. Young children could bring new bobbins for the machines, girls helped their mothers work the looms, and boys helped their fathers operate, repair, and clean the heaviest equipment.

But most mill jobs were intended for young unmarried girls. Such girls might be orphans like Hannah Canaday in this story. Others left their families, went away to work in factories, and saved their earnings to help at home.

Mill girls earned about $2 a week for working six long days. Like Hannie, they lived in boarding-houses near the mill. Four or five girls shared one bedroom, and everyone ate meals together at the boardinghouse.

The First Factories

Until the early 1800s, most everyday things were made at home. America had no factories. But that changed almost overnight, when the British stopped shipping goods to America during the War of 1812. To continue getting what they needed, businessmen in New England built brick factories and began producing goods by machine.

Textile mills sprang up rapidly beside New England rivers, to weave cloth from the cotton grown on southern farms. By the 1830s, the fabric industry brought greater wealth to the region than any other kind of manufacturing. At first, mill towns seemed ideal. The mill company provided jobs, housing, stores, and sometimes recreation and education to its workers. But as machines were improved to run faster and produce more, working conditions grew unsafe and unbearable.

Down she went with a splash.

low to watch, forgetting her long skirts. Just then, the factory bell had rung in the distance. Hannie started back, but her foot slid into a pocket of mud. Down she went with a splash. She had no other work clothes, so she went dripping back to the mill. When she arrived, she learned the punishment for being late. The doors were locked, and no one heard her calling. Her place at the bobbins was vacant, and her name had been written on a slate for all to see.

Anxiously, she had returned to her boardinghouse. Mrs. Miller was chopping beef for supper. She was not very friendly. She said that going to the marsh was foolish. But she found Hannie some dry clothes and let her help peel potatoes.

The next morning, Wednesday, she had hurried to the mill to begin work. When she arrived, Mr. Stewart had spoken sharply to her. He said she could be fired if she were late once more.

Now Hannie was locked out again. She hated the mill. Tomorrow she would probably lose her job. Suddenly she decided to go get her baby mouse and run away. Maybe she could sneak back to the boardinghouse and climb the stairs without being seen.

A few minutes later, as Hannie passed the row of company stores, she saw Mrs. Miller in the boardinghouse yard, tossing a pail of scraps to the chickens. Quickly the little girl slipped into a shop. It was a small bookstore lined with neat shelves. A slender man wearing a striped vest and wire eyeglasses sat writing at a desk.

"Good afternoon, Miss. May I help you find something?" he asked. Hannie's face felt hot. Oh yes, she thought. Find me a basket to hide under.

"Er, yes . . . I mean . . . no! But I do thank you." Hannie lifted the sides of her apron and curtsied. She had never done such a thing before, but she thought it was how you answered a gentleman. She turned toward a shelf. The letters on the books meant nothing to her.

The shopkeeper approached. Hannie saw that he was hiding a smile. She pointed to a small red book.

"I've decided—after all—this one will do nicely."

"Oh," he replied, taking the book with surprise. "I'm glad to sell this. Almost no one reads Greek anymore. This is thirty cents."

Thinking quickly, Hannie asked him to hold it for two weeks. "I've just begun working. I'll soon have plenty of money for books. I love books."

"Certainly, my dear, I'll gladly hold it. Tell me your name and I'll keep it right here." He began wrapping the book in paper.

"Hannah Canaday," she answered proudly.

The shopkeeper raised an eyebrow. "Do you room at Mrs. Miller's?" he asked.

Hannie hesitated. Lying was wrong, but admitting that she lived at the boarding-house would make it clear that she was a mill girl—and locked out.

"I hate the mill," she blurted out suddenly. "I hate the bells, and I hate Mr. Stewart. And I *don't* love books. I can't even read!"

"Come, sit down. Let's have a talk." The shopkeeper drew a chair beside his own and sat down.

"I think I've already heard something about your adventures," he said. "You like the marsh, don't you? My children do, too. We walk there every Saturday." He continued, "My name is James Stewart. My brother David owns the mill. Perhaps we will find him later, when you feel better. Maybe I can help you."

Hannie knew he couldn't, but she listened anyway. *This* Mr. Stewart was kind. He told her that during the winter, he was the schoolmaster. He owned the bookshop, too. After his brother had built the mill and hired the girls, he had offered to teach reading. He had a class of nine girls, who were on their second book.

Mr. Stewart stopped talking and reached for Hannie's book. He unwrapped it.

"I have one you might like better, Hannah," he said. "This is my gift to you." He handed her another book. "I hope you will join our reading group."

Hannie could hardly believe it. A book of her own! She opened it carefully. Above the words, each page had an animal drawing. Hannie recognized muskrats, beavers, ducks, and others.

"Thank you!" she breathed.

Mr. Stewart smiled. "Bring your book, my friend, and come with me to the mill. I think my brother will let you finish your work today."

What About the Boys?

For a long time in America, married women couldn't have their own jobs—except for raising children and running the house—as they do today. A wife could help with her husband's business, but many other jobs were off limits to her. (Ask what kind of work your grandmothers and great-grandmothers have done in their lifetimes. They might surprise you.)

In the 1800s the habit of a young woman going away to work in a factory was something new and unusual. To help it seem safe and proper, the mill company—just like companies today—tried to present a good image to the community.

Why weren't the boys working in the factories, too? Some were. But if you guessed that most of them were at home, helping their fathers on the farm, learning a trade, or going to school, you guessed right.

Hannie could hardly believe it. A book of her own!

Make a Mill Doll

With a few scraps of fabric and a little time, you can make and dress a doll in clothing that girls like Hannie wore to the factory. Sew the doll by hand, or ask a friend or family member for help with a sewing machine.

What You Need:

Paper to make a pattern; scissors; unbleached muslin; some ribbon (¼ inch wide); matching thread; 1 ounce curly yarn (hair color); a needle; straight pins; a small bag of cotton balls for stuffing; a piece of small-print fabric for a dress; buttons and lace (optional); and a fine-tipped black marker to draw a face.

1. Make a pattern for the doll's head and body, arms, and legs with all the markings, using the illustration as a guide. (If you make the head and body 5 inches tall, the arms 3 inches long, and the legs 4 inches long, the doll will be about 9 inches tall.) Remember to add ¼ inch around all your pattern pieces; this is the cutting line. Cut out your pattern. Fold the muslin in half. Lay the pattern pieces on the muslin with the arrows following the straight grain of the fabric. Pin each piece and cut it out, cutting through both pieces of fabric at once.

2. Remove the pins from the pattern, and save it to use again. Match the two head-and-body pieces together, and pin them again. Taking small stitches with your needle and thread, begin at a lower corner of the doll's body and sew a seam ¼ inch inside the edge of

the fabric, sewing around the head and down the other side, leaving holes where the arms will be attached. Leave the bottom edge unstitched. Carefully turn the head and body right side out (a chopstick will help you) and stuff it with cotton.

3. Follow the directions in step two for cutting and sewing each arm and leg piece. (Be sure to cut four arm and four leg pieces.) Leave the ends unstitched for stuffing. Turn each piece inside out. Stuff them with cotton balls and sew them closed.

4. Attach the arms to the doll's body by stuffing the ends into the holes, and sew the arms in place. Pin the legs in place, turn the edges under, and sew together the bottom edges of the doll, sewing the legs in place as you go.

5. To make the hair, loop the yarn around a 7-inch piece of cardboard. Tie a knot around the middle of the yarn at the top of the cardboard. Slide the yarn off the cardboard, keeping it in a loop. Snip the loop to make one bundle of hair. With needle and thread, sew the hair onto the top of the doll's head. Spread it out to cover the back of the head, and stitch it at the back of the neck to hold it in place. If you like, tie it with a ribbon, or draw it back into a bun, as factory girls wore it so it wouldn't catch in the machines.

6. Practice drawing the doll's eyes and mouth on a scrap of muslin, and then draw them on the doll. You can use markers or fabric paints to make rosy cheeks and freckles on your doll.

7. To make the dress and apron, use the same process as you did for the doll. Using the illustration as a guide, draw a pattern. Cut the pattern out, and pin it onto the fabric. Cut the dress from a double piece so it has both a front and a back. Cut the apron from a single layer of scrap muslin. Sew the dress along the sewing line, and turn it right side out. Turn the neck opening, sleeves, and bottom edge under, and hem the edges. Hem the edges of the apron as well. Cut the ribbon into four equal pieces, and stitch each one to the apron where the pattern is marked.

8. Dress the doll by putting the dress over her head. Gather the front of the dress into folds, and place the apron over the dress, tying it in back with the ribbon. Trim the ribbon ends if they are too long. Add lace, buttons, and other details to the dress and apron if you like. Enjoy your new doll!

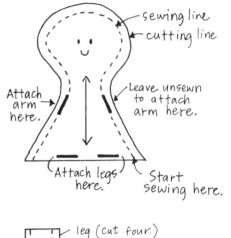

sewing line
cutting line
Attach arm here.
Leave unsewn to attach arm here.
Attach legs here.
Start sewing here.

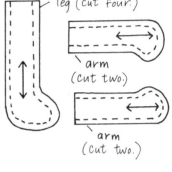

leg (cut four.)
arm (cut two.)
arm (cut two.)

dress (cut two.)

apron (cut one.)

for the hair:

Cut yarn here.

Sew hair onto head.

Families waited eagerly for the peddler's visit.

MILL BELLS

The alarm clock that awakened mill girls every morning was a loud bell that sounded from the roof of the factory. It began ringing loudly at 4:30 A.M. The mill girls scrambled to be at the factory by 5:00. They worked for two and a half hours before they were sent back to their boardinghouses to eat breakfast at 7:30 A.M.

At noon the bells rang to tell them they had one half hour to eat lunch—always at the boardinghouse—and get back to work on time. If they were just one minute late, as Hannie was, they found the huge wooden mill doors already locked, and they could be fired.

On dark winter nights, the factory was lit by candles. Mill girls stayed at work until the bell rang at 7:30 P.M. each evening. Then they went home to the boardinghouse for supper. After supper, they could visit with each other, read, sew, or go to the shops near the mill.

The last bell of the day rang at 9:30 P.M., when every girl was expected to be in bed. Seven hours later, the morning bell rang and the new day began, exactly like the day before.

On Sundays, girls were expected to attend church. After that, they could do as they pleased. This usually meant doing laundry, mending, or reading. Girls who had families might spend the time writing letters to send home.

YANKEE PEDDLERS

At nineteen, James Guild of Vermont called himself an "unhappy farmer boy" trapped in a life of hoeing and axing. One day he packed some things in a little trunk and set out for New York. Along the way he knocked on doors, showing people the needles and threads, buttons and trinkets they could buy from him.

When he didn't grow rich this way, Jim bought a soldering iron and became a repairman. He walked as far as Ohio and South Carolina, fixing things and playing the tambourine for pennies.

Today some people might think of Jim Guild as homeless. But in the nineteenth century, these wandering salesmen were called "Yankee peddlers" (because most were from New England states). They were important to America's business life. Their wagons or trunks were crammed with books, tinware, tools, perfumes, and other new American products, and they were welcomed in isolated areas.

Families who might have to travel many miles to a store waited eagerly for the peddler's visit, crowding around his wagon to see what amazing things he brought.

Have you ever gone up and down your street selling candy bars or chocolates to raise money for sports or school? If so, you know about peddlers. The Yankee peddler was America's first traveling salesman.

Wild in America

After the Revolution, Americans felt proud and independent. They had won the war against great odds. For many, life was more comfortable. Parents became less strict with their children.

Some Europeans were shocked by the behavior of American children. An Englishwoman said that American parents made their children show off for company. If the children weren't home, the parents dragged out their portraits instead. Someone else complained that the minute they could talk, children argued with their parents. A French count remarked that "a child of the lower classes" leaves his parents "almost like the animal does."

Maybe it was a child running free on the prairie that caused a traveling Englishman to say that in America, "Baby citizens are allowed to run wild . . . and do whatever they please."

Jason and the Mustangs

He twirled the rope over his head.

Going Ahead in Texas

Texas was a part of the nation of Mexico in 1821. That same year, Mexican officials allowed an American named Stephen Austin to bring 300 families from the United States to live on Mexican land.

Stephen Austin respected Mexican society. He wanted the people of his settlement to obey Mexican laws and be loyal to the Mexican government.

Austin's settlement wasn't the last. Other Americans soon formed settlements on Mexican land. People came from Tennessee, the Carolinas, Mississippi, and New York. By 1830, there were 16,000 Americans living in Texas. There were four times as many Americans living in Texas as there were Mexicans.

These new settlements were filled with ambitious people called "Go Aheads." They were rugged and independent and disliked following any rules except their own.

"See those mustangs," said Matthew Archer, looking out at the Texan prairie.

"I see them," said his son, Jason.

"The troop has stopped. Go ahead," urged the father. "Rope yourself one." He removed his buckskin hat and slapped it against his son's horse.

Jason's horse jolted forward. He guided his horse near the mustangs. He stopped twenty feet from the troop. The mustangs became nervous. They cocked their heads and flared their nostrils.

The boy calmed his horse and studied the troop, looking for a mustang to rope. He settled on one with a brown coat and white spots. Jason had his prey. Now he had to capture it.

Jason dug the spurs on his boots into his horse. The horse charged the mustangs, and they bolted. The boy chased after his chosen horse.

While gripping the reins in his left hand, Jason picked up his ox-hide lasso tied to the saddle. He twirled the rope over his head, waiting for the right moment to release the lasso's loop. He was so nervous he forgot to breathe.

Jason cast the lasso's loop. It sailed through the air and landed around the mustang's neck. He pulled hard on his reins, braking his horse.

The angry mustang bucked and stood on its back legs. The boy turned his horse toward his father. He dug his spurs into his horse and raced off, dragging the mustang behind him.

Matthew Archer howled for joy as his son approached. Jason had roped his first mustang.

That night, wrapped in Mexican blankets, they celebrated by the cooking fire. They feasted on venison and honey. The father took out his harmonica and made it sing with his breath.

Suddenly Matthew stopped playing. "Did you hear that?" asked the father. "Might be that panther again. Go check the pen gate."

Jason checked the pen. It was filled with fifty mustangs. Tomorrow he and his father would go into the town of Goliad and sell them. The mustangs would be slaughtered, and the meat sold. Their skins would be tanned, and their manes and tails would be turned into rope.

Jason trotted back to his father. He watched as he fired his rifle into the darkness.

"That should keep that varmint away. Let's get inside."

They walked inside their oak-log cabin. Matthew shut the door, and Jason closed the wooden shutters to keep out the bugs and the cold.

In the corner of the room was one bed. Its frame was notched into the walls and was held up by one pole dug into the dirt floor. The father and son lay down on the rawhide straps that crisscrossed the frame and covered themselves with their smoke-scented blankets.

They didn't wash up. They didn't care to. They were content to bathe and change their clothes every six months.

"Do you miss Tennessee?" asked the son.

"Nah. I miss your mother, rest her soul. But I'll find another wife soon enough. Tomorrow we'll go ahead and bring in some horses and get some money. Soon we'll buy us some cattle."

"Tomorrow night there's going to be fandango dancing on the plaza," said the son.

"Those Mexican dances ain't no pigeon's wing. Don't be concerning yourself with those Mexicans. They're going back to Mexico soon enough."

"But this is Mexico," replied the son.

"Not for long, son, not for long."

In the corner of the room was one bed.

Giving Directions

When a stranger asked a Texian woman how to get to Colonel Rivers's place—just five miles away—this is what he was told:

"Do you see that lone tree out yander in the perara [prairie]? Well, keep straight on to that tree, and arter you pass it 'bout fifty or maybe so a hundred yards, you will come to a cow trail, but don't take that; go right straight across it, and purty soon you come to another; follow that till you git to whar it splits, then take the right hand, or ruther, I say the left hand split, and it'll carry you into the road to Thompson's Mill . . . and when you git to the mill road, follow that till it splits—but you keep the straight forward split to whar it strikes the bottom, and there it sprangles off, so I can't say adzackly which split you do take. Howsomever, 'taint fur, anyway, from there to Col. Rivers, and I reckon you won't go wrong."

In February of 1836, the Alamo was surrounded by Mexican troops. Inside, 180 Texans defended the fort they had taken about a year earlier from the Mexicans. For ten days, within the Alamo's crumbling walls, the Texans withstood the Mexican attack. When the Alamo finally fell, almost all the Texans were killed. Their deaths weren't forgotten. Texans shouted "Remember the Alamo!" as they attacked and defeated the Mexican army in the final battle of the Texas war for independence, at the San Jacinto River.

TEXAS REBELS

Americans swarmed into Texas. Many of them were foreigners living illegally on Mexican land.

Most settlers ignored Mexicans living in Texas. They also ignored Mexican laws. Settlers brought slaves with them, even though Mexican law forbade slavery. Mexican law required everyone to pay a duty on goods brought in from the U.S. The Americans refused.

Many of the laws that the settlers disliked were repealed by the Mexican government. However, when Antonio López de Santa Anna declared himself Mexico's new ruler, in the early 1830s, he reinstated the repealed laws.

The settlers were furious. In every settlement, Americans set up committees to organize fighting units and to communicate with each other.

After a group of Texan rebels attacked a Mexican fort, delegates from twelve communities met to decide how to coordinate their actions. They created a list of reasons for taking up arms against the Mexican government. But the delegates also agreed that a peaceful solution should be found to resolve the settlers' complaints.

By 1835, the delegates felt they had no choice but to declare war on Mexico. They wrote a constitution and created a government. On March 2, 1836, Texas announced its independence from Mexico.

On April 21, the newly formed Texan army, headed by Sam Houston, defeated General Santa Anna's army at the San Jacinto River. Texas became an independent country, the Republic of Texas.

The Texan victory over Mexico didn't end the conflict, though. Many Texans wanted Texas to become part of the United States. Mexico vowed to declare war on the United States if Texas became a U.S. state.

When James K. Polk became president, in 1844, he didn't care about Mexico's threat of war. He believed that it was America's "Manifest Destiny" to settle all the land between the Atlantic and the Pacific Oceans.

In 1845 Texas became part of the United States. Mexico and the U.S. argued over the correct border. This annoyed President Polk. He was already irritated by Mexico's refusal to sell the territory it held in the Southwest and California. Polk sent an army to the Rio Grande near the border between Texas and Mexico. Gunfire soon was exchanged.

The United States declared war on Mexico in 1846. After months of bloody fighting, the two nations signed a peace treaty on February 2, 1848. In the treaty of Guadalupe Hidalgo, the U.S. agreed to pay Mexico $15 million. In exchange, Mexico ceded to the U.S. over 500,000 square miles of its territory. This vast land included all or parts of the future states of California, Nevada, Utah, Arizona, New Mexico, Colorado, and Wyoming.

The war was a disaster for Mexico. For the United States, it was a triumph. Just ten days before the treaty was signed, a discovery was made along a rushing river in California that would bring untold riches to the American people and untold thousands to the West. Do you know what it was?

RIDING CONTEST IN SAN ANTONIO

An author named John Duvall saw a riding contest in San Antonio. This is some of what he saw:

"The next morning we found . . . men, women, and children all preparing to leave for the scene of the great riding match which was to take place in the prairie. . . . Gaily dressed 'caballeros' [Mexican cowboys] were prancing along the street on their gaudily caparisoned [elaborately draped] steeds; Rangers [citizen-soldiers] mounted on their horses and dressed in buckskin hunting shirts, leggins, and slouched hats and with pistols and bowie knives stuck in their belts, galloped here and there among the crowd. . . .

"We followed the crowd until we came to San Pedro. . . . Drawn up in line on one side of the arena and sitting like statues upon their horses were the Comanche Warriors, decked out in their savage finery of paints, feathers, and beads. . . . Opposite to them, drawn up in single file also, was their old enemies . . . the Texas Rangers, and a few Mexican rancheros [ranchers], dressed in their steeple-crown, broad-brim sombreros, showy scarfs, and slashed trousers. . . .

"The show began. A Mexican lad mounted on a pony with a spear in his hand, cantered off a couple of hundred yards and laid the spear flat on the ground. Immediately, a Comanche brave started forth from their line and plunging his spurs into his horse's flanks dashed off in a direction opposite to that where the spear was lying . . . then wheeling suddenly he came rushing back at full speed, and as he passed the spot where the spear had been placed . . . he swung from his saddle, seized the spear . . . continued . . . for some distance . . . galloped back (dropping the spear as he returned at the same spot from which he had taken it).

"The same feat was then performed by a dozen or so each of the Rangers, rancheros, and Indians. . . . A glove was then substituted in place of the spear, and in like manner it was picked up from the ground by the riders, whilst going at full speed. . . .

"A board with a bull's eye marked upon it was then set up. . . . A warrior with his bow in his hand and three or four arrows . . . charged full speed towards the mark and in the little time he was passing it planted two arrows in the board. The Rangers and the rancheros then took their turn using their pistols. . . .

"A good many other extraordinary feats were performed such as hanging by one leg to the horn of the saddle in such a way that the rider could not be seen by those he was supposed to be charging and whilst in that position discharging pistols or shooting arrows at an imaginary foe under the horse's neck; jumping from the horse when at a gallop, running a few steps by his side, and springing back into the saddle again without checking him for a moment; passing under the horse's neck and coming up into the saddle again from the opposite side, etc.— all performed while the horse was running. No feats of horsemanship we had ever seen exhibited . . . could compare with them."

The Man Who Slept in Two Places

There was an independent man nicknamed "Old Single." He hated the idea of Texas being annexed, or joined, to the U.S. "Blast their skins," he said. "I don't care ef tha does annexate Texas! . . . I'll quit and go to Arkansas wher a decent white man kin live 'thout being pestered."

Old Single did move to Arkansas, but before he did, he lived on the dividing line between Texas and the U.S. When he slept, half of him slept in Texas and the other half slept in the U.S.

"A good many other extraordinary feats were performed".

Can You Spin a Rope?

The rope was an important tool to the Mexican and the American cowboy. Besides roping mustangs, many cowboys rounded up cattle that roamed over hundreds of miles of land. This event was called a *rodeo*, the Spanish word for a roundup.

The cattle were driven back to the ranch. The cowboys used a lasso, or rope, to catch the cattle to be taken to market and calves to be branded.

Roping cattle and mustangs takes great skill. Just being able to spin a rope takes time and patience. You'll see when you try it.

What You Need:

A 14-foot braided rope and some electrical, masking, or duct tape.

1. Take one end of the rope, and make a small honda, or loop, by bending the rope back on itself. Use tape to hold the loop in place.

2. Take the other end of the rope, thread it through the honda, and make a loop. The loop should be about 6 inches in diameter.

3. Hold the loop in one hand with the honda positioned toward the ground.

4. Gather about 3 feet of the extra rope and hold it in the same hand.

5. Stand tall, feet apart, and begin spinning the rope in a forward, or clockwise, direction.

6. When you feel you've created a comfortable rhythm, release the extra rope and continue spinning the loop. To help keep the rope from kinking up, don't hold the rope tightly. Let the rope turn in your hand.

When you have the hang of it, increase the diameter of the loop. Feel confident? Spin the rope ever higher in the air. Set up targets and try to lasso them. Happy roping, cowboys and cowgirls!

Tape rope to make a honda.

Audubon's Assistant

John James Audubon had a dream. He wanted to paint an exact likeness of every bird that lived in the United States. In October 1820, Audubon traveled by flatboat to explore the Mississippi and westward.

Audubon traveled with his assistant Joseph Mason. Though he was only thirteen years old, Mason was a skilled painter of plant life, and he would get better under Audubon's instruction.

No matter where Audubon was, he took detailed notes of the birds he observed. Until then, most Americans had no interest in birds except to eat them or occasionally find pleasure in their songs.

Audubon found enjoyment in studying, naming, and amassing as much information about the birds of the United States as he could. When he found a new bird, he attempted to paint it. First he shot the bird. Then he attached the bird's body to the inside of a wooden box with wire. The box's opening was covered with wires placed in rows and columns, forming a grid of squares.

Audubon sat in front of this box with a piece of white paper. On this paper he drew the same pattern of squares that covered the box.

Whichever part of the bird appeared in each square of the box's grid, that was what he drew on the same square of the grid on his paper. He used a ruler and a pair of calipers to assure accuracy. Using this system, Audubon was able to create an accurate, life-size painting of the bird.

You can do the same with plant life. You can be Joseph Mason.

You Will Need:

Plant specimens, a shoe box (including the cover), straight pins, a clear sheet of acetate, white drawing paper, pencils, a permanent marker (black), a ruler, scissors, a caliper or compass, and watercolor paints and brushes.

1. Find a flower, a plant, a tree leaf—something that is unfamiliar or interesting to you.
2. If your specimen is small, pin it to the back of the shoe box cover. If your specimen is larger, pin it to the back of the shoe box.
3. Cut the sheet of acetate so that it is the same size as the box or the cover.
4. Draw horizontal lines on this section of acetate, with your marker, from the top to the bottom. If the specimen is small, the lines should be ½ inch apart. If the specimen is large, the lines should be 1 inch apart.
5. Draw vertical lines on this same section. These lines should also be either ½ or 1 inch apart. When you are through, you will have a grid of squares.
6. Draw this same grid of squares onto your drawing paper, using your pencil. Don't make the grid lines too dark.
7. Place the section of acetate over the box or cover.
8. Draw the specimen. Don't bear down on your pencil! Use a ruler and a caliper or a compass to help you create an accurate drawing. This is not a quick task. It takes focus and patience.
9. Paint the sketch, and place your signature in the corner.
10. After you've finished your painting, find out everything you can about your specimen. Look in a gardening book, or find a book in the library on plants and flowers.
11. Mount and frame your finished work.

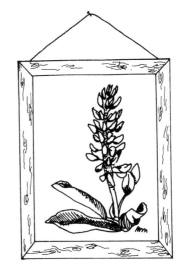

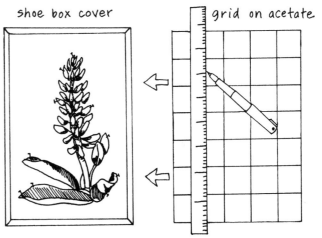

shoe box cover   grid on acetate

Put grid over shoe box to help you draw accurately.

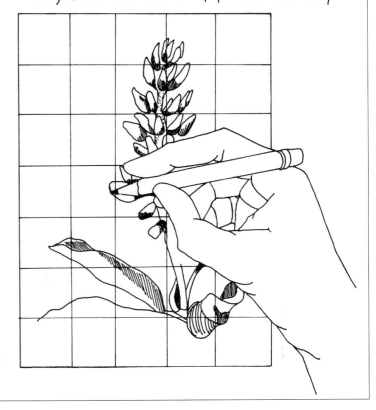

The Hero of Harvard

The small flame from the oil lamp flickered yellow and blue. Richard Henry Dana Jr. reached over his Latin book to turn the lamp up brighter. The light illuminated his cluttered room in Cambridge, Massachusetts. Books and papers were piled high beside him. Others were stacked on the table beside his bed.

Richard couldn't concentrate on his homework. He was graduating from college in June and he knew he should be studying. But his thoughts kept drifting away from school. When he closed his eyes, he imagined he was once again sailing on a great ship over the Pacific Ocean, and he saw the smooth golden hills of California just as they had looked to him.

Opening the drawer in his desk, Richard drew out his little diary. For two years at sea, it had been a good friend. In it he described turning from a seasick student into a serious sailor. He had witnessed some cruelties toward men that he would never forget. But he had also enjoyed the pleasant towns and friendly people of Mexican California. His diary told all this.

Richard had worked hard from 1834 to 1836, loading the ship with hundreds of stiff, dirty cowhides that would make fine leather shoes and purses in Boston. The weather on the Pacific Coast seemed ideal to him, and the bays and natural harbors were beautiful. It was a country that most Americans knew nothing about.

As he daydreamed, Richard thought about the questions his friends had asked. They wanted to know what it was like to be a sailor and live at sea. They had kidded him, calling him the "hero of Harvard," but he knew their teasing was mixed with admiration.

Suddenly Richard closed his diary. He realized he had a story to tell. He had already written most of it. But it wasn't quite finished. He wanted people to know how a cruel sea captain could treat his men, and how unjust it was to the sailors. He would turn his diary into a book that everyone could read.

Richard Henry Dana Jr. called his book Two Years Before the Mast. *It was published in 1840, three years after he graduated from college. It did help change laws and protect sailors. (It also described California favorably, as a place of good harbors, rich soil, and excellent weather.) Richard became a lawyer and spent his life fighting social injustices. Here are some excerpts from* Two Years Before the Mast.

"Wednesday, Nov. 5th, 1834—Just before eight o'clock . . . the cry of 'All hands ahoy!' was sounded down . . . the . . . hatchway, and hurrying upon deck, we found a large black cloud rolling on toward us from the south-west, and blackening the whole heavens. 'Here comes Cape Horn!' said the chief mate; and we had hardly time to haul down and clew up before it was upon us. . . . In a few moments a heavier sea was raised than I had ever seen before, and as it was directly ahead, the little brig [ship] . . . plunged into it, and all the forward part of her was under water; the sea pouring in through the bow-ports and hawse-hole . . . threatening to wash everything overboard. In the lee scuppers it was up to a man's waist. . . . Throughout the night it stormed violently—rain, hail, snow, and sleet beating upon the vessel—the wind contin-uing ahead, and the sea running high. At daybreak . . . the deck was covered with snow.

"Monday, Nov. 19th. This was a black day in our calendar. At seven o'clock in the morning, it being our watch below, we were aroused from a sound sleep by the cry of 'All hands ahoy! a man overboard!' This unwonted cry sent a thrill through the heart of everyone, and . . . it was not until out upon the wide Pacific in our little boat that I knew whom we had lost. It was George Ballmer, a young English sailor, who was prized by the officers as an active and willing seaman, and by the crew as a lively hearty fellow, and a good shipmate. . . . He fell from the starboard . . . shrouds [rigging], and not knowing how to swim, and being heavily dressed, with all those things round his neck, he probably sank immediately. . . .

"Thursday, Dec. 25th. This day was Christmas, but it brought us no holiday. The only change was that we had a plum duff [flatcake] for dinner, and the crew quarrelled with the steward because he did not give us our usual allowance of molasses to eat with it. He thought the plums would be a substitute for the molasses, but we were not to be cheated out of our rights in this way.

"Friday, May 8th, 1835. Arrived at San Diego. Here we found the little harbor deserted . . . anything in the way of variety I liked. . . . I stood on the beach while the brig got under weigh, and watched her until she rounded the point, and then went up to the hide-house to take up my quarters for a few months. . . .

"Here was a change in my life as complete as it had been sudden. In the twinkling of an eye, I was transformed from a sailor into a 'beachcomber' and a hide curer; yet the novelty and the . . . independence of the life were not unpleasant. Our hide-house was a large building, made of rough boards, and intended to hold forty thousand hides. In one corner of it, a small room was parted off, in which four berths were made, where we were to live, with mother earth for our floor. It contained a table, a small locker for pots, spoons, plates, etc., and a small hole cut to let in the light. Here we put our chests, threw our bedding into the berths, and took up our quarters. . . .

"The morning after my landing, I began the duties of hide-curing. . . . The first thing is to put them in soak. This is done by carrying them down at low tide, and making them fast, in small piles, by ropes, and letting the tide come up and cover them. . . . There they lie forty-eight hours, when they are taken out, and rolled up, in wheelbarrows, and thrown into the vats. These vats contain brine . . . being sea-water, with great quantities of salt thrown in. This pickles the hides. . . . From these vats they are taken, and . . . spread upon the ground, and carefully . . . stretched . . . so that they may

"The morning after my landing, I began the duties of hide-curing."

dry smooth. After they were staked, and while yet wet and soft, we used to go upon them with our knives, and carefully cut off all the bad parts:—the pieces of meat and fat, which would . . . infect the whole if stowed away in a vessel for many months. . . . This was the most difficult part of our duty. . . . It was also a long process, as six of us had to clean an hundred and fifty. . . . The first day, I was so slow and awkward that I cleaned only eight . . . and in . . . three weeks, could keep up with the others, and clean my proportion—twenty-five.

"On Saturday night, the hides, in every stage of progress, are carefully covered up, and not uncovered until Monday morning. On Sundays we had absolutely no work to do, unless it was to kill a bullock, which was sent down for our use about once a week. . . . Another good arrangement was, that we had just so much work to do, and when that was through, the time was our own. Knowing this, we worked hard. . . . By this means we had about three hours to our-

selves every afternoon; and at sundown we had our supper, and our work was done for the day. . . . [In the afternoons I generally read, wrote, and made or mended clothes]. . . . The evenings we generally spent at one or another's houses, and I often went up and spent an hour or so at the over; which was called the . . . "Oahu Coffee-house". . . .

"Sunday, December 27th [1835]. We had now finished all our business at this port [now called San Francisco], and it being Sunday, we unmoored ship and got under weigh, firing a salute to the Russian brig, and another to the Presidio, which were both answered. . . .

"If California ever becomes a prosperous country, this bay will be the centre of its prosperity. The abundance of wood and water, the extreme fertility of its shores, the excellence of its climate, which is as near to being perfect as any in the world . . . all fit it for a place of great importance; and indeed, it has attracted much attention."

The Spanish Empire in the West

In 1796 the Spanish government reluctantly let an American ship drop anchor along the California coast. The *Otter*, sailed by Captain Ebenezer Dorr, was the first U.S. ship that Spain permitted to stop in Monterey Bay.

Spain was not happy to see British, Russian, and American sailors load their ships with sea otter pelts, as the *Otter* did, and sail away to China, where the furs brought fat profits.

But the California shoreline stretched over a thousand miles, and it couldn't be patrolled. There were only five Spanish *presidios*, or forts, at San Diego, Los Angeles, Santa Barbara, Monterey, and San Francisco, to protect hundreds of miles of coast. It would have been impossible to keep foreigners out, but Spain did not give up happily.

"We unmoored ship and got under weigh."

WHAT AMERICA'S FIRST BOOKWORMS READ

Do you remember the story of Rip Van Winkle, the man who slept for twenty years, or Ichabod Crane and the "Legend of Sleepy Hollow"? Both stories were written by a curly-haired, handsome young man who was born in 1783, the year the Revolutionary War ended. To honor George Washington for his victory, the boy's mother named her son Washington Irving.

Like most young Americans, Irving grew up reading the Holy Bible and popular British novels, such as *Pilgrim's Progress*.

He went to law school to please his parents, but he loved the theatre more than anything. He was nineteen when he wrote his first lively essays for a newspaper. His humor included a silly history of New York. In it he said that the women of Manhattan were so busy scrubbing and mopping, they grew to have webbed fingers like a duck, and if you could check, you would see that they also had mermaid tails. Irving

wrote seriously, too, about Christopher Columbus and George Washington. In the 1830s he traveled in the West and wrote *A Tour on the Prairies*. His writing was very popular, and he is considered one of America's first great authors.

James Fenimore Cooper was six years younger than Irving, and did not become a writer until he was an adult. He grew up near Cooperstown, New York (his father laid out the town), surrounded by wilderness. He loved hunting, fishing, and hearing stories about the Indians who once lived nearby. Cooper created a frontier character with the odd name of Natty Bumppo. Five novels tell the story of Bumppo's life. *The Last of the Mohicans*, second in the series, is still popular as a book and also as a movie. Cooper wrote more than thirty novels and other books. He was the first important American writer to describe the mountains, forests, plains, and rivers of America in colorful detail. His stories are well-told adventures, full of bravery and danger. Cooper is often considered America's first great novelist.

The Devil and Tom Walker

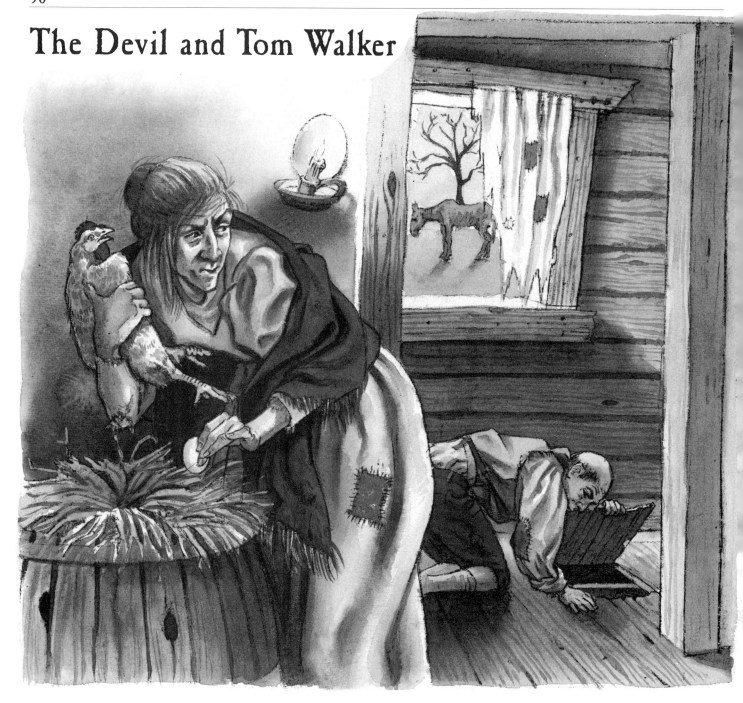

whatever the woman could lay hands on, she hid away.

This story, by Washington Irving, appeared in his book Tales of a Traveller, *published in 1824. Parts of the story's beginning are printed here. To find out how it ends, ask your librarian to help you find a copy of the book.*

"About the year 1727, just at the time that earthquakes were prevalent in New England, and shook many tall sinners down upon their knees, there lived near this place a meager, miserly fellow, of the name of Tom Walker. He had a wife as miserly as himself; they were so miserly that they even conspired to cheat each other. Whatever the woman could lay hands on, she hid away; a hen could not cackle but she was on the alert to secure the new-laid egg. Her husband was continually prying about to detect her secret hoards, and many and fierce were the conflicts that took place about what ought to have been common property.

"They lived in a forlorn-looking house that stood alone, and had an air of starvation. A few straggling savin trees, emblems of sterility, grew near it; no smoke ever curled from its chimney; no traveller stopped at its door. A miserable horse, whose ribs were as articulate as the bars of a gridiron, stalked about a field, where a thin carpet of moss, scarcely covering the ragged beds of pudding stone, tantalized and balked his hunger; and sometimes he would lean his head over the fence, look piteously at the passer-by, and seem to petition deliverance from this land of famine.

"The house and its inmates had altogether a bad name. Tom's wife was a tall termagant, fierce of temper, loud of tongue, and strong of arm. Her voice was often heard in wordy warfare with her husband; and his face sometimes showed signs that their conflicts were not confined to words. No one ventured, however, to interfere between them. The lonely wayfarer shrunk within himself at the horrid clamor and clapper-clawing, eyed the den of discord askance; and hurried on his way. . . .

"One day that Tom Walker had been to a distant part of the neighborhood, he took what he considered a short cut homeward, through the swamp. Like most short cuts, it was an ill-chosen route. The swamp was thickly grown with great gloomy pines and hemlocks, some of them ninety feet high, which made it dark at noonday and a retreat for all the owls of the neighborhood. It was full of pits and quagmires,

partly covered with weeds and mosses, where the green surface often betrayed the traveller into a gulf of black, smothering mud; there were also dark and stagnant pools, the abodes of the tadpole, the bullfrog, and the water snake, where the trunks of pines and hemlocks lay half-drowned, half-rotting, looking like alligators sleeping in the mire. . . .

"Tom Walker, however, was not a man to be troubled with any fears of the kind. He reposed himself for some time on the trunk of a fallen hemlock, listening to the boding cry of the tree toad, and delving with his walking staff into a mound of black mold at his feet. As he turned up the soil unconsciously, his staff struck against something hard. He raked it out of the vegetable mold, and lo! a cloven skull, with an Indian tomahawk buried deep in it, lay before him. The rust on the weapon showed the time that had elapsed since this deathblow had been given. It was a dreary memento of the fierce struggle that had taken place in this last foothold of the Indian warriors. Humph! said Tom Walker as he gave it a kick to shake the dirt from it.

"'Let that skull alone!' said a gruff voice. Tom lifted his eyes and beheld a great black man seated directly opposite him, on the stump of a tree. . . ."

"Let that skull alone!"

If You Want to Know More

This book is over, but you don't have to stop. There's so much more to learn. You've just skimmed the top. Our nation has many more stories for you. There's more to do, if you want to have fun. Below you'll find books to read, crafts to make, and trips to take. And remember, for history's sake, take the time to see that as each day passes, you make history, too.

Books

To learn more about working in a textile mill, find the book *Lyddie*, by Katherine Paterson (New York: Lodestar Books, 1991). In this story, a young Vermont farm girl hires on at a textile factory, hoping to save enough money to help her family. But along the way, her troubles multiply as she fights the unhealthy conditions in the factory.

Did you know Benjamin Franklin was carried to the Constitutional Convention on a sedan chair by four prisoners? These and other fun facts are woven into a lively telling of the convention in *Shh! We're Writing the Constitution*, by Jean Fritz (New York: G.P. Putnam's Sons, 1987). Don't miss this one!

Lewis and Clark's cross-country experiences are difficult to imagine today. They wrote their journals in an old-fashioned style that may be hard to follow, but give it a try with *The Journals of Lewis and Clark*, edited by Bernard DeVoto (Boston: Houghton Mifflin, 1953). Or read *Lewis and Clark and the Route to the Pacific*, by Seamus Cazan (New York: Chelsea House, 1991) or *Sacajawea, Indian Interpreter to Lewis and Clark*, by Marion Brown (Chicago: Childrens Press, 1988). Both are written for modern kids.

Beyond the Rocky Mountains there was a new land, a new adventure. It was the Pacific Northwest. The Oregon Trail could take you there, if you dared. The Oregon Trail stretched across the Great Plains and the Rocky Mountains to Oregon and California. Along the way there were wild waters to cross and life-threatening diseases. Every traveler feared "seeing the elephant," or the worst possible conditions. *The Oregon Trail*, by Leonard Everett Fisher (New York: Holiday House, 1990), with its photos and traveler descriptions, will immerse you in this wondrous and dangerous world.

Sometimes it's hard to imagine the United States 200 years ago. People were beginning traditions, such as the presidential inauguration, or inventing engine-driven boats. Today we take these things for granted.

Imagine Benjamin Banneker taking the time to study and figure out when a sunrise and a sunset would occur. If you'd like to explore the night sky for yourself, find *The Glow-in-the-Dark Night Sky Book*, by Clint Hatchett (New York: Random House, 1988). Its phosphorescent charts of the universe are keyed to the seasons in the United States. All you need is a flashlight to recharge the maps. Head outside at night and you'll soon know what Banneker must have felt like.

What tools did a cowboy use? What did he wear? What did he do for fun? What did the cowboy do during the winter? If you have a question about cowboys, *The Cowboy Trade* (New York: Holiday House, 1972) will most likely have your answer. You can round up this book at your library.

Crafts and Projects

If you enjoy making models, you will have fun with *Historic Models of Early America and How to Make Them*, by C. J. Maginley (New York: Harcourt Brace & Company, 1947). It has instructions for making a plow, an ox cart, a steamboat, a Conestoga wagon, and many other models of articles that Americans used in the past. The book lists the tools you will need, the best wood to use, how to finish your models, and includes general tips about the projects. If you aren't an experienced carpenter, you will need the help of a grown-up.

Historical Sites

Pioneer living is alive! In the Conner Prairie Pioneer Settlement in Noblesville, Indiana, you can speak with the people of 1836. Walk into a house, the log cabin schoolhouse, the blacksmith shop, or the general store. Talk with people playing the parts of Indiana set-tlers. They are more than happy to tell you about their occupation and their families. And if that's not enough, head to the Pioneer Adventure Center, where you can take part in activities such as weaving, quilting, or a game of quoits. Quoits is similar to horseshoes, only a ring of rope, or a flattened ring of iron, is tossed instead of horseshoes. The Conner Prairie Pioneer Settlement is open Tuesday to Sunday, May through October. For information, call (317) 773-3633.

Want to take a canal boat ride? Where? At Roscoe Village. This village is an 1830s canal town located in Coshocton, Ohio. You can take a forty-five-minute canal boat ride, or take a walk on a one-mile renewed section of the Ohio and Erie Canal. For more information, call (614) 622-9310.

There are also pioneer villages in eastern states. What was a dressmaker's shop or a doctor's office like in the 1800s? In New York you can find out at the Genesee Country Museum, in Rochester, New York. For more information, call (716) 538-6822.

Walk back in time on the streets of Harrisville, New Hampshire, and see what a textile factory was really like. The entire village has been named an historic landmark. In the town center visit the Harris Mill, built over Goose Creek. The historic district also contains the Cheshire Mills, private homes, and churches you can explore.

In the South, see how Texan pioneers lived at Log Cabin Village, in Fort Worth, Texas. For more information, call (817) 926-5881. Visit the battleground of the final fight for Texan independence at San Jacinto, *Sam Houston Park*, twenty-one miles east of Houston, Texas. For more information, call (713) 479-2431.

If you're traveling in Washington state, take time to visit the Lewis and Clark Interpretive Center, at Fort Canby State Park in Ilwaco, off Highway 101. This is where the explorers first laid eyes on the "great Pacific Ocian." Follow the exhibit to a window that gives you a spectacular view of the ocean. The center is free and open daily. For more information, call (206) 642-3078.

Do you want to know more about Cherokee life? You can visit the Oconaluftee Indian Village and the Museum of the Cherokee Indian, in Cherokee, North Carolina. From mid-June to late August, the Cherokee Historical Association presents "Unto These Hills." This outdoor dramatic presentation tells the life of the Cherokee people, including the "Trail of Tears," also known as "The Trail Where They Wept." For information, call (704) 497-2111.

"The most historic square mile in America." That is Independence National Historical Park, in Philadelphia, Pennsylvania. Step back in time when you enter Independence Hall or the Pennsylvania State House. It was here that the delegates drafted the Constitution. It was also here that the Declaration of Independence was signed. Everywhere you turn in this park there is American history waiting to be discovered. Don't miss Carpenters' Hall, where the first Continental Congress met, or Franklin Court, where you can learn all about the brilliant Benjamin Franklin.

This historic park is very popular. If you want to avoid the crowds, arrive early, or plan for a weekday visit. For more information, call (215) 627-1776.

How about Washington, D.C.? This city is chock-full of historic places to explore, such as the White House and the Library of Congress. How do you make up your mind what to visit? Let a book be your guide—*A Kid's Guide to Washington, D.C.*, by Diane C. Clark (San Diego: Gulliver Books, Harcourt Brace & Company, 1989). This book is a powerhouse of historical facts, fun stories, places to go, games, and visitor information.

Independence Hall

Roscoe Village

Log Cabin Village

Conner Prairie

Sam Houston Park

Index